HEALTHY EATING ON A  BUDGET

Dexter Poin

Hey everyone, it is now July of 2017, and I am updating this book. Thanks for checking out my book I really appreciate it. I hope that you can find the information in it to be of great value to you as you are choosing to focus on your health by choosing to eat right all while being on a very strict budget. I have lived on a strict budget myself and have done so for my entire life, all while still trying to choose the healthiest foods in order to fuel my body. I packed a lot of information in here and made sure that I intertwined as best as I could the balancing act of living on a budget all while still trying to eat like a thoroughbred race horse. My entire life has changed so much, since writing this book, from my sisters garage, where I was living at the time. Without getting into it here, my diet has also changed a bit. I am more plant based than ever these days, and focus on my "3 ILES", which I also do not have time to get into here. But basically, I dedicate my every waking moment, to improving myself, from the inside out. There is so much of this stuff in here, that cannot be found anywhere. That is why I wrote it probably. I thank you for ordering this book, and want to see you find your "zone". Whatever that means?!

Carpe diem.

Dexter

Table of Contents

Introduction: why I wrote this 9

We are what we eat. 14

Staples: 30

Complex carbohydrate staples sources: 37

Fruit: 50

Vegetables: 57

Protein: 61

Fats: 85

Condiments: 100

Calorie counting and macros: 105

Blueberry smoothie recipes 143

Banana Mango 150

Banana & Dates 151

Banana Dates & Pineapple 153

Cranberry Hone 155

Peanut Butter & Fruit 157

Oat Smoothie 159

Icey Dates 161

Banana Raisins 163

Cinnamon Raisin 165

Mango Heavy 167

Blueberry Cinnamon 168

Almond Milk Strawberry 169

Mango Berry Cinnamon 170

How to shop and eat right for under 50$ a week: 176

Prepare your food ahead of time: 189

Conclusion: 191

Fruit and Bean Quinoa Salad 194

Cranberry Kale Quinoa 197

Easy Quinoa Porridge 199

Simple Garlic Quinoa 201

Quinoa Broccoli Casserole 203

Healthy Quinoa Salad 205

Blueberry Breakfast Quinoa 207

Green Beans Quinoa 209

Tasty Red Quinoa with Rice 211

Kale Raisin Quinoa 213

Mixed Vegetable Quinoa 215

Delicious Lentil Quinoa 217

Yummy Fruit and Quinoa Salad 219

Spinach kale Chickpeas Quinoa 221

Pomegranate Mint Quinoa Salad 223

Turmeric Curry Quinoa 225

Easy Steel Cut Oats 227

Simple Plain Quinoa 229

Yummy Apple Quinoa 231

Introduction: why I wrote this

So you want to learn how to *eat healthy* on a budget do yea? Well you have come to the right place my friends because this is absolutely the story of my entire life. I may not know much, but if there is something that I do know, it is that I do know how to eat right.

I am also poor as well and have been for most of my life. I have always figured out a way to eat healthy foods on a very small budget.

I know that some of you probably do not believe me when I say that I am poor right? I know that I wouldn't believe me. I know that a lot of people tend to say a lot of things in order to sell you on something, am I right?

I personally know people who make over 100 thousand dollars a year and joke around about being poor. A lot of people use that as a way to cut tension in conversations with people who are really poor. I personally do not care what others make but I know that the subject of what people make for a living makes people act weird around others who are of a different income class than they are.

Trust me when I say that I am currently living below the poverty level and was raised my entire life below the poverty level. I am actually very much used to it. I had a span of about a decade or so when I had my own business and also worked in a trade where I made some pretty good money as far as lower middle class individuals go.

But circumstances changed and so did my wants and desires in life. About 4 years ago I got out of the business that I had been in for 15 years and started doing something that paid me far less money than I was making in order to go to school and try to get into an actual career type of job which I could be proud of.

I actually didn't enroll in school until 2 years ago as I spent two years trying to figure out exactly what it was that I wanted to do with my life.

But I am still in school now, and still trying to get into the Fire Department at age 37. And I don't plan on giving up any time soon either. I work a pretty medial job doing watch repair. I am not telling you this so that you can feel bad for me for being broke. Please do not think that I am. I do not accept peoples pity because I do not pity my own self.

I am **CHOOSING** to live this way so that I have a chance at a future with some real promise. I also have another very small side gig as I like to call it that is sort of related to the books I write in the health/nutrition/fitness industry *(or whatever it is that you want to call it. I call it a scam)*. Although I have not yet decided if I want to go public with it as I am happy right now with just a very small clientele.

If I start getting into my 40s and find out that my Fire Department dreams just weren't meant to be then I will reevaluate and find something else to dream about. But to be honest I am not yet looking that far into the future.

I sort of believe in living every single day as if it were a brand new beginning. I could go outside tomorrow and get side swiped by a car and be bed ridden for the rest of my life. I would then have to figure out how to dust myself off and get back in the game of life. All while being on my back in a bed somewhere. Or I could just let myself wither away and die a slow suffering death feeling sorry for myself. Those would be the only two choices that I would present myself with in that specific scenario.

So please do not think that I am trying to give you a boohoo sob story here because I am actually the happiest that I have ever been in my entire life.

I feel liberated and free as I pretty much am doing what I want when I want. Which sometimes I think about it and laugh, that with my nomad type of personality that doesn't exactly conform to anything, I am trying to get into the Fire Department where it is all about conforming and doing exactly as you are told *(sir yes sir)*. But I am actually willing to suck up my pride and put up with all of that BS as I am doing this for other reasons that are more important to me than stroking my ego.

What I am actually trying to do here by telling you this is to motivate you to get focused on what is really important in life. Food is not just a big part of my life. ***It is the main part of my life.*** It is the reason that I am able to do some of the things that I can still do at age 37. 37 is not old by any means, but I am able to still do things athletically that most people would absolutely not be able to do at 37.

This is all due to nutrition. Ok genetics has a lot to do with it to. Actually genetics has more to do with it than does nutrition but once you start to get up past a certain age, if the nutrition is not spot on then even the best genetics in the world will start to crumble and wither away.

We are what we eat.

I have said this many times that we are not when we eat, we are what we eat. This is not going to be a preachy diet and health book but I will say a few things that I believe are important for people to know when it comes to proper nutrition for the body.

This book is about how to eat healthy on a budget. I would never write a book just about how to eat cheap. That is easy actually. Just eat prison spreads and drink King Cobra malt liquor.

And watch your genetics slowly begin to wither away.

So this is going to be a little bit of a combo here. You are not only going to get information on how to eat healthy with a very limited amount of money to spend on food.

You are also going to get my point of views on the subject of nutrition, diet, and even fitness, sprinkled all in at the most inopportune moments as I tend to type without a backspace button whatever pops into my head at the moment. I never write anything with an outline. If I tried I would still be on the first 20 words on my first book scratching my head and picking my nose.

Most people don't even have a clue what eating healthy even is. I am not saying that people have to try and emulate the way that I eat to a gnats nose. But what most people consider to be healthy food choices, even moderately healthy food choices are very far from it.

I don't know what your specific situation is. I don't know if you are a college kid trying to just learn how to eat reasonably healthy while on a budget. Or if you are a single mother of 4 who is trying to juggle raising your kids and work all at the same time and looking for a way to feed your family healthy foods on a very limited income.

Well since that college "kid"(37 year old kid here) is me, and that single mother of 4 was my mom, I am going to try to find a happy medium here for everyone who is wanting to learn how to eat like a Thoroughbred race horse and feel vibrant all while living on a very fixed income.

This is going to be geared for everyone. All ages and all life situations can benefit from the things that I am going to tell you here.

I was very fortunate to have somewhat of a hippy minded kind of mom. My mom is not a bra burning hairy legged tree worshiping hippy no. I actually tease her about being a hippy when she really is not what most people would consider a hippy to be. Those people are the fake hippies that actually make a bad name and ruin the good causes that they leach onto for political reasons.

But all of these things that these phony 21st century hippies are making money with hand over fist by pushing on the general public of dolts, and convincing people that are now "miracle foods" that can reverse the aging process and cure future diseases that haven't even been invented yet. My **"MUM"** (as a friend has now got me calling my mom) was doing all of that hippy stuff when I was a little kid and even before I was born.

My **"MUM"** was cooking with coconut oil ever since I could remember. Long before it ever became the cure for everything under, over, around, and directly through the sun.

In fact the latest news that I heard about the all amazing coconut oil was that it cured Superman from his intolerance to kryptonite. Who would have thought that a three table spoon enema of extra virgin *(pun intended)* coconut oil with a turkey baster was all that was needed for Superman to be able to survive around kryptonite. Unfortunately for Superman he needs a dose every three hours or its effectiveness will begin to wear off.

Oy Vey, I forgot my **"MUM"** is probably reading this. Sorry **"MUM"**. Its ok folks she knows how I am. She has probably heard me say this stupid Superman joke more times than she can count.

But seriously, my mom was using coconut oil when I was a small child. She was using stevia before it ever became ridiculously overpriced and hard to find a brand that is actually 100% stevia without any kind of chemical sweetener filler along with it.

I grew up as a kid on sun tea with 100% stevia as a sweetener in the summer time while all of my friends had their little Hi – C and Capri Suns they would devour by the dozens. Remember Capri Suns with the tiny little straw that you have to poke through the even tinier little hole and break through the stupidly shaped container, or whatever the heck that thing is called because its not called a cup or a bottle?

All the kids would waste about half of it as they would squeeze on the soft container or whatever you want to call it all while trying to poke the little straw into that tiny little hole. I used to see kids at school get so frustrated with that little hole that they would actually start stabbing it in. They were probably going through sugar withdrawals and were desperately trying to get their fix like a crack addict.

I had a friend as a kid that I used to be so jealous of his life. The poor kid was obese ever since I met him in probably the 1st grade. His parents are to blame as they let him eat anything that his clogged up heart desired to eat. And when I say anything I mean anything.

They were both obese themselves and had their own business and were pretty well off for where we lived. They were well off enough to buy all of the name brand junk foods and frozen foods such as hot pockets and hungry mans and things of this nature. Actually the most nutritious thing that this kid would eat would be his 6 frozen chimichanga microwavable burritos after school.

I never seen one piece of fruit inside of their house. Not one, ever. In fact, I swear that I am not making this up. This kid was an only child so he had his own bedroom that he slept in, and also had another bedroom that he had dedicated to candy. Yes you read that right, he had his other bedroom all decorated and loaded with candy of all kinds.

Remember Charlie and the Chocolate Factory? No, not the stupid one with the idiot who was pretending to be Michael Jackson pretending to be Willie Wonka. The good one with old grandpa Joe and Veruca who *"wants it nooooooooooooooooooooooooooooooooow"*.

Well remember the scene were all of the kids go into the candy store and the creepy pedophile looking man with a weird looking part in the middle of his greasy hair begins to sing to the children as he lures them into his trap by throwing candy at them from a ladder on rollers?

Well this kids room looked a lot like that candy store. His parents owned a store that sold items having to do with childrens parties. They had clowns that worked for them and all that good stuff.

So this kid basically lived like a spoiled oompa loompa where he was surrounded by candy along with toys and whatever else that goes a long with childrens parties.

I would go over his house and hang out with him and be so jealous that he got to eat foods like Captain Crunch cereal, and Pop Tarts, and Twinkies, and Gummy Bears, and Nerds. Remember nerds? He used to eat a box of nerds in one mouth full. He would fill his mouth with pop rocks and carbonated soda and make his mouth foam like a dog with rabies.

I was not allowed to eat any of that stuff. But come on, I was a kid and of course when I went over to his house I would partake of the forbidden fruit from time to time. Well maybe fruit wasn't the best word of choice but I think that you get what I am implying.

Well the cats out of the bag now! Sorry **"MUM"** but I did cave into peer pressure some of the times and did my best to turn myself into a diabetic by splurging on a mix of Skittles, Starburst, and Cactus Cooler. I had always felt as if I were doing something illegal though. In my house this type of behavior actually would have been considered illegal. My mom would occasionally make a homemade cake and every now and again when the moon was blue I remember we would get to have root beer floats. But all this stuff was on very rare occasion.

My mom would feed us liver! Come on liver! Hahahaha! I don't eat cow anymore for my own reasons but back in the 80s our meats weren't loaded as much with all of the hormones that they are today. Me and my siblings still make jokes around my mom about eating liver for dinner. And of course she cooked it in nothing but its own juices which were about as juicy as the sole of a Wolverine work boot.

My friend a few blocks over was eating a big punch bowl of Count Chocodiles, meanwhile I was at my house eating a mix of boiled beans, brown rice with vegetables, and a beef liver steak. All while washing it down with a nice tall glass of plain water.

At the time I was so jealous of my friend. I thought that he had life by the tail. Now as an adult I am so thankful to my mom that she instilled in me good eating habits that many of them I still use to this day.

I have since taken what she instilled in me and stepped things up a few notches to where now I am known as the crazy loony tune in my circle of people around me.

So like I said earlier, this is going to kind of be a universal type of eating on a budget book that everyone can hopefully get some use out of no matter what their life schedule is like.

I am going to for the most part personalize this and show you the foods that I eat and how I buy my foods and even prepare some of my meals. But I will add some other suggestions as well on other types of healthy foods that people can use in their meals that I don't particularly eat. Or I at least don't eat too often.

Remember just because you are broke does not mean that you have to eat badly. If you are a single person like myself with no kids to worry about keeping alive and well, then there really is no excuse for you. If you are the single mom that I was talking about with your kids being your number one priority over everything in your life then you obviously are going to have to really stretch out everything that you can out of the foods that you prepare for your family.

I know how it is to not have much to work with when it comes to food. I am going to do the best I can here to help those who are trying to cook healthy for multiple people as well as the dumb college kid who has a hard time boiling water.

By the time you are done reading this I personally hope that everyone can take with them the importance of proper nutrition in our lives. Most people just really do not value the importance of nutrition. I don't get how so many people don't take nutrition seriously and understand that without proper nutrition then everything else in our lives will begin to fall apart.

What we eat really should be the foundation of our existence. This should be the reason why we wake up in the morning to go out and live life to its fullest.

Our number one instinct is to search for food and water. Not shelter, not clothing, not sex, and definitely not money.

Now in the modern world we have been spoiled enough to be able to take for granted the fact that food will be provided for most of us even the poor. At least in a country like where I live which is in the United States.

There are other people in other countries who are not so fortunate even in this day and age which I find disgusting. So you mean to tell me that there are people who get paid millions and millions of dollars to **PLAY** a sport that they just so happened to be born with the genetics to excel in, while there are millions and millions of other people all over the world who are so malnourished and dehydrated they cant even produce saliva from their mouths?

This world is a joke.

This is why I quit watching sports a handful of years ago completely. I cant stomach watching a thug who whines and cries about everything getting worshiped and treated as if they are Gods because they **PLAY** a game that entertains the room temperature IQ crowd who guzzles down Budweiser and lives their life through these clowns. You can call me names if you want to but this is the way I now see things.

Like I have said before in other books I removed my back space button so everything that I am thinking

in my head at the time I type it down and it stays no matter what.

My books are monologues not Wikipedia reports.

So in other countries were these people have not been desensitized by the insane world that all of us have to live in they still are relying on their natural instincts.

And the bodies first natural instinct of choice is to survive. You must eat or you wont survive. The human body is pretty amazing. The body will find a way to survive off of kitty litter if it had to. I am not sure how long it will survive for but the body will do its best to stay alive as long as possible I promise you that.

I have read some pretty sad, and interesting, and also disgusting stories all at the same time of things that people ate to survive during the Holocaust. If you ever get a chance try and look some of that stuff up.

As sad as those kind of stories are they are also very motivating to me in a certain way as all those people who have suffered like that are true survivors in every sense of the word. People like me don't have a clue what suffering is in comparison to people who have suffered through real hardships.

There are people now still suffering in similar ways. I need to keep these kind of thoughts at least in the middle of my mind in order for me to not get too caught up in this dumb ass world and just be thankful for all that I have which a lot in comparison to many people all around the globe.

I shop at Traders Joes for crying out loud.

I own a refrigerator.

I own a vehicle.

I own a nice cell phone and have 3 laptops for crying out loud I am not really poor.

I have no clue how all of you are going to read this. I am guessing that many of you have already deleted this eBook from your Kindle app and are on my review page right now leaving me a nice big fat stinky **0** star review with a big gigantic piece of your mind. That's cool, you deserve to vent your problems on someone I suppose. I would rather it be me instead of your mailman or something.

Staples:

Staples should be the meat and potatoes (pun intended) of every single persons diet whether they are on a budget or not. We all should have our same basic staples that we eat every single day of our lives like clockwork according to our bodies specific needs.

Note as I purposely did not say wants and needs, I just said needs.

Forget what you want. It is not about what you want it is only about what your specific body needs to survive and run like a well oiled machine on all cylinders. We are all genetically different and have different genes that cause our bodies to run better on some sources of fuel than others.

You may run better on a higher carbohydrate diet coming from complex carbohydrate sources such as oats, and brown rice. While Spanky down the street may run better on a moderate carbohydrate diet coming from sources that are still low on the glycemic index but higher in sugars such as fruits.

All of this stuff is sprinkled into my other books so if you want to know more, then you can go check them out. But I will delve into it a little bit here as well.

A carbohydrate is absolutely not just a carbohydrate.

It is somewhat of a new fad these days in certain sectors of this industry and certainly not this one but more so in the bodybuilding sector primarily where children give other advice to children on YouTube to teach that all carbs are the same as they enter the body.

This is just stupid and I don't know what they all are trying to sell but you can bet that the people spreading this joke around are indeed trying to sell some kind of eating pattern or diet plan. They are all fads to me. It does not matter what the pattern or plan, they are all just nothing but fads that will be here for a while and then be gone tomorrow.

On the other hand, I also believe that so many people are so messed up and know so little about nutrition that they absolutely need some kind of bandwagon to jump onto in order for them to eat in a way that is reasonably healthy.

Unfortunately they will always be having to find new bandwagons to jump onto for the rest of their lives unless they take the time to get the desire to want to learn about exactly what their bodies need to run on a full tank and feel at their best.

Who wants to eat reasonably healthy anyways? I don't. But unfortunately the overwhelming majority of people do want to eat just reasonably healthy and if they need to jump on a fad like Paleo, or what have you I am all for that and wish them well.

I really do hope that some of you people who know absolutely nothing about nutrition are in here conversating with me. Because If you are then by the time you are finished reading this you will at least know the basics of how to figure out your calories and macronutrient breakdown of those calories.

Just learning this one little thing will put you on the right track towards optimum health. You will be able to spend less money on your food all while choosing the foods that **YOUR** body needs.

This will really make my day!

I constantly say this and I purposely sound like a broken record with this but I am not a self proclaimed guru or a wannabe coach of any kind. I am not trying to build my little cult. I just want to help people learn the very basics that I believe should be taught in every school.

I am not bragging but I know more about nutrition than most Dieticians (I know that sounds arrogant, but I am just being honest). Sure they know the jargon and are skilled in the art of touting long winded verbiage that means a hill of beans out in the **REAL WORLD** where we all live in.

But look at them. Are they in any kind of shape other than the shape of round? Most of them are 20%+ body fat. They only recite what was washed into their brains. And legally they cannot sway from this either.

This is why the majority of people who know their stuff would never want to be a Dietician. I am not knocking them but a lot of them just simply want the title and love to be in a position of authority.

You also have got to go through a lot of years of brainwashing in order to become a registered Dietician. I do tip my hats off to them for that. They dedicated their lives to earning this title.

Then you have got *"Nutritionist's"*. Oy vey, don't even get me started on them. If you had a week to spare I could fill it bagging on Nutritionist's. Those certificates are just falling out of Cracker Jack boxes now days.

I even seen some lady one time at Walmart pull out 5, Yes 5 Nutritionist certificates from just one Cracker Jack box. She was so excited she ran out of the store and forgot to grab her 20 tubs of Ben & Jerry's ice cream that she had sitting at the cash register. I guess she felt like it was high time that she started practicing what she would soon to be preaching now that she was a brand new Nutritionist. X 5.

Anyways, so where was I?

Oh yea, I was talking about staples.

I think that I was about to go off on a rant about carbohydrates but then I got sidetracked from my first sidetrack. That happens to me a lot. I think I will save the carbohydrate rant for another time. Which may even be further down in this book who knows?

But since we are sort of on the subject of carbohydrates, we will start there with our staples conversation.

Complex carbohydrate staples sources:

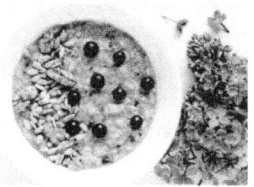

Carbohydrates get a bad rap these days and take the blame for a lot of our generations fat problems. It is true that the wrong type of carbs for certain people will be part of the cause of their issues with body fat. But many diet plans seem to overlook so many other issues and seem to try and convince uninformed people that it is all carbohydrates fault for why they are fat.

This is wrong.

Carbohydrates = energy

No carbohydrates = no energy

It is as simple as that. If you want to be active and vibrant, then you need to get the right amount of carbohydrates in your system from the **PROPER SOURCES.** If you want to be sedated and do nothing more than walk from your couch to your refrigerator, then go and try all of those low to no carb fad diets. It is very possible to lose scale weight on low carb high fat diets with zero exercise. If this is the life that you want to lead, then by all means go and dive right into those types of diets.

But be prepared to abandon ship at some point because these types of diets simply are just not sustainable for **moderately healthy individuals.**

Someone who suffers from some kind of an illness that is forcing them to eat a specific way is an entirely different conversation. One that I am not qualified to, or even want to discuss.

I am talking about moderately healthy individuals who are battling to keep the dunlap belly from dunlapping any further over their belt.

So what I am going to do here is I am going to give you all some good sources of carbohydrate staples that I believe that everyone should at least find two of them and implement them in their life daily.

These sources are all easy on the pocket book and should be bought in bulk at whatever your local big lot type of market is where you live. I am not affiliated at all with this company but just last year I discovered what Smart and Final was. My **MUM** had been telling me to go and shop there for food for several years but I never listened to her for some dumb reason. Anyways, I now get all of my bulk carb foods from there. It is like a little mini Costco. If you have one of them in your city I would say go and check out what they have.

Eating super healthy is actually cheaper than eating bad processed foods.

I just don't understand how so many people absolutely do not know this. I suppose that when you get raised on the foods that my friend that I mentioned earlier was raised on, then you are sort of entering the race of life with both shoe laces tied together and an extra load to carry on your back.

This just doesn't seem fair to me.

Like I said earlier I believe that every child should be taught the basics of nutrition in school. But unfortunately this would probably open up a stinky can of worms as those people who would be teaching the basics don't even know the basics themselves.

There is no one size fits all, and the basics has to be a broad stroked reference point at which everyone can use to start from and then apply what works for their bodies needs. This is why I don't like all of these fads because they are basically a one size fits all plan. Even when they say they aren't they still are trust me. It is all about money anyways, and people will say anything when it comes to making money. Don't trust anyone in this industry, not even me.

Let me first start out by telling you my carbohydrate sources of choice. These are the

carbohydrates that I use as fuel for my body every single day of my life like clockwork.

So how many of you bet that I was going to start off with oats? Come on, you knew that I was going to say oats. That is the number one breakfast of champions right there folks.

Well not just oats by themselves but oats are a staple in my diet. I eat oats along with some other things within about 15 minutes of waking up every single morning. I never get bored of it either because food is fuel to me not something I do for entertainment. I view eating as the process of survival.

Go ahead and laugh at me I don't care. I laugh at myself all day long. But I also can go my entire life without ever even craving a single piece of *"junk"* food not ever. This does not mean that I don't occasionally have foods that are considered *"junk"*. But I absolutely do not have cravings for them ever.

Think about it, how hard would it be for most people to eliminate processed foods from their lives completely? Pretty hard, and outright impossible for many people. So there has got to be something to my philosophy of how I view food.

I am just saying what I do. You can do whatever floats your boat.

JEEZ LOUISE OATS ARE PROCESSED?!!!!

Hahahaha, yes oats are processed so I already have contradicted myself right off the bat by saying things like eliminate processed foods which we all should. There is a reason why I like to contradict myself. It is to show that we as humans do need flexibility in our lives or we will burst.

Old Fashioned rolled oats from the goofy looking Quaker guy with the funny white hair dew and hat on are a type of processed food that I will allow myself to consume on a daily basis.

Just about every single thing that we eat are processed when you really get down to the nitty gritty of things. Even our vegetables and fruits are considered **"processed".**

Oats are something that is very good for you and also can be purchased in bulk for very cheap. I would go with the old fashioned oats instead of the minute oats. And definitely stay away from oats with added flavoring of any kind. You cant buy those oats in bulk anyways and that is the main purpose of what we are talking about here.

When I talk about condiments I will talk about ways to make your oats taste better without adding any kind of granulated sugar or chemical sweeteners for sugar replacements.

My other two carbohydrate staples that I rotate them both into my eating patterns are brown rice and either yams, or sweet potatoes.

I just bought a 25 lb. bag of brown rice for 15$. This is going to last me quite a while as I am only feeding 1 which is me, although I pretty much eat for 2.

You obviously cant buy yams and sweet potatoes in bulk or they will rot on you but I like to throw a handful of yam meals into my weekly feedings just to break up the monotony of brown rice every single day which if I had to I would have no problem eating. Keep an eye out on my Authors page on Amazon for my yam smoothie recipe book coming out very soon. I will put out some YouTube videos showing how easy it is to make them as well.

With the exception of my fruit that I eat these three carbohydrate sources are basically where I get the bulk of my carbohydrates from.

Other sources of inexpensive carbohydrates that you can buy in bulk and wont go bad that are high on the nutritional side of things are:

Lentils

Split peas

Quinoa

Black beans

Kidney beans

Garbanzo beans

And pretty much just about any other type of bean that you enjoy. Years ago I used to be really against canned beans. But I have since found a brand that doesn't contain too many of the extra ingredients that I am not looking for to add into my diet. Always check the labels on anything that is canned that you buy. Anything from a can is always going to have a preservative in it of some kind. We want to stay away from preservatives as much as possible, but

when you are on a budget sometimes you have got to do what you have got to do in order to survive.

In the winter time I will occasionally want to enjoy a soup that I make that is a 3 to 1 ratio of split pea to lentils. Why don't I just give you the stupid little recipe right now.

- **Boil your split peas until they are cooked (duh).**
- **Boil your lentils until they are cooked (I am master of the obvious huh?).**
- **I like to boil them with a little garlic and chopped up red onion. I add the garlic in from the beginning, and add the onion in at the end of the cooking process.**
- **Cook your salmon with no oils until it is charcoal black (If you actually do this then you probably should not be near a stove).**
- **Then I just make one big goulash and add in whatever else I have in my refrigerator like**

- **cilantro, white onion and chives, red cabbage, and sometimes a little baby spinach.**
- **As far as seasoning goes I am sort of a black pepper guy myself, but I do enjoy Mrs. Dash as well.**

I don't need to fancy things up so sorry if my recipe is stupid, but it really does taste good, especially on a nice cold day. It is a nutritious meal as well. I also will balance out my macronutrient breakdown and make enough for me to get at least two whole meals out of it.

I will show you a very easy way how to figure out your calories and macronutrients later. This is very important to our overall health and many people don't even know where to even begin when it comes to figuring out how to count calories properly.

When people talk about being frugal with their money, or being poor, or being broke, what is the first thing that usually comes up in the conversation when it comes to what foods they will be eating? I guess it depends on your culture, but some people will say rice and beans, which is ok I suppose but doesn't have to be the only foods you can afford.

But where I am from most people will say they will now have to be eating a diet that consists mainly of Top Ramen and canned tuna.

Top Ramen is not as cheap as people think it is, and it definitely holds absolutely no nutritional value whatsoever. I wouldn't feed Top Ramen to a stray dog that I found on the freeway. I am not joking, I would feel bad if I fed a dog this. There are a lot of things that humans eat that I wouldn't feed to stray dog, like all fast foods.

One of the carb sources that I mentioned above should be in your daily meals. At least in 1 or 2 of those meals, at least.

Fruit:

I am a big fruit eater, I love me some fruit of all kinds. But fruit can get pretty expensive depending on where you live. And organic fruit can be ridiculously expensive and more than likely if you are on a budget you wont be able to even think about going organic.

It is kind of sad how organic has become so popular now days that they have decided to make it only affordable for those who are well off.

But do not fret young grasshopper, because us poor people can still find ways to eat organic if we so choose to do so. We just have got to be smart about which types of foods that we are going to be choosing to consume that are organic.

With all those complex carb sources that I was talking about earlier you are pretty much not going to be able to afford organic. Unless you shop smartly and come across sales on organic brown rice, or organic lentils and so on, you are going to be ok without going organic with those types of foods.

When it comes to fruit be a little bit pickier on which fruits you will be able to afford and also which organic fruits you will be able to afford.

You will have your staple fruits that are cheap like bananas which you don't need to worry so much about buying organic when it comes to bananas as you would if you were buying a fruit like blueberries, or strawberries as they have no peeling like the bananas do.

The easy way to decide what you should and shouldn't buy organic is to just go by the skin or the peeling of the fruit. If the peeling is thick like a banana or an orange then you are ok not getting organic.

But things such as berries are out in the elements and are not protected from pesticides and whatever else gets sprayed on these things these days so trying your best to buy organic would be a better choice should you be able to afford to do so.

This is all according to your budget.

Here is what I do.

I eat fruits of all kinds, but my main fruit that I eat every single day of my life is blueberries. I also eat bananas most days of the week, but if I only had to have one fruit it would be blueberries for a number of reasons and all of them pretty much being nutritional reasons. Although I do love the taste of blueberries but it is not about taste to me.

I buy *flash frozen* fruits and would encourage people to do so also. Not just fruits either, but also vegetables as well. But always read the labels first. Not so much with flash frozen vegetables, but with fruits some brands mainly the more popular brands will add sugar and preservatives to the fruit. So I always check the package and make sure that there is only one ingredient and that is whatever type of fruit it is that is in the package.

I personally cannot afford to always buy organic blueberries, especially considering how much of them that I eat. I have actually bought only organic blueberries before for a while and tried to penny pinch in other areas, but in the long run it just was not worth doing for me.

So what I do is I just add one organic package to every 3 or 4 non organic packages that I buy. This way I am still getting at least some of my blueberries organic and at least making my mind feel better as if I am doing something right I suppose. Who knows, organic anything may even be a scam these days am I right? The whole organic movement has become too corporate for me and I smell a rat. But I still try and lean organic if at all possible. It cant hurt anything other than my wallet.

I do it anyways just to set my mind at ease. But if I am really strapped for cash then I will just go with the non organic.

Always try and get in at least a couple of pieces of fruit into your daily meals. It doesn't really matter which type of fruit you eat just as long as you are getting fruit into your diet.

Shop smart when it comes to fruit and look for sales. I know that where I live when the bananas start to go spotted they will discount them by half the price. The perfect time to eat bananas actually is when they are spotted. Most people don't know that and think that they look gross, but they actually are sweeter when they are spotted.

If you are ridiculously picky and cant stand spotted bananas then freeze them and blend them up in smoothies. I have got some smoothie recipe books if you want to know some good smoothie recipes that I use myself. Go check them out on my Authors page on Amazon if you wish. Both of them have made best sellers lists (which doesn't mean squat to you), and every single smoothie recipe I put into a book I have not only tried, but I have made up for myself. I was making smoothies way before all of these bandwagon jumpers decided to jump onto the smoothie fad.

If you are someone who craves refined sugars and processed foods then fruit is the only answer to combat those cravings. If you need to, constantly switch up your fruits so that you can get a wide variety of flavors onto your pallet. Like I said, I buy flash frozen fruits all the time. The best fruits that I usually come across that are flash frozen are:

Blueberries

Mangos

Strawberries

Pineapple

Figs

Cherries

Raspberries

And snozberries

Who here has ever heard of a snozberry?

I have done the math and in my opinion at least where I live, all of these types of fruits that I mentioned above seem to be far less expensive when they are flash frozen. They also will last a whole lot longer as well.

Remember fruit is your friend. Get in as much fruit into your body as you can possibly afford and reap the benefits from doing so.

Vegetables:

Never, ever, ever count your vegetables (with rare exceptions) as part of your caloric intake for the day, but eat an abundance of them. This is my motto when it comes to vegetables, and I have explained why I feel this way in other books but I will not explain it here.

I believe in eating as many vegetables as you can. But I do not believe in counting the calories or the macronutrients as part of your daily intake. To me vegetables are an extra bonus.

I am poor and I eat a butt load of vegetables daily.

Vegetables are my filler food as I have a very huge appetite. If it weren't for vegetables I would probably over load on carbohydrates and be a fat blob like many people in this country.

Vegetables are another food that I buy flash frozen some of the time. My favorite flash frozen vegetables are:

Green beans

Broccoli

Spinach

Bell peppers

Peas

Sweet corn

Later I will throw out some ideas for you on how I mix my vegetables into my meals. I switch up my vegetables all the time and pretty much just eat which ever ones that I have whenever I have them. I don't assign certain vegetables with certain meals. With the exception being smoothies. I like to put baby spinach into my smoothies pretty much most of the time.

I will occasionally make broccoli smoothies, and put bell peppers into my smoothies. But for the most part I go with the baby spinach.

In my smoothie recipe books I make fun of the new praying mantic colored smoothie fad that is going around these days.

If you are a smoothie lover then you might find those books informative and a little bit entertaining as well. Like I said, I run far away from fads, and there are so many smoothie fads these days that are duping people into believing that blending your fruits and vegetables unleashes super human powers from the nectar of the Gods.

We are such a gullible species.

I am a huge salad eater. I eat at least one, and sometimes three huge salads a day with my meals. Iceberg lettuce is not the most nutrient dense lettuces out there, but it is cheap and tastes really great. I mix my lettuces and use iceberg for filler in order to get my salads to be huge and filling. I also like crunchy things and iceberg lettuce is very crunchy.

I eat my salads out of a plastic Tupperware container about the size of a shoe box if this gives you any indication to how big my salads are.

Vegetables are your friend not your enemy, so eat as much of them as you can afford. Try the method of using vegetables as filler, especially if your appetite is huge like mine is, or if you are hooked on refined over processed foods.

Protein:

Yes protein, your most expensive staple. Everyone has a different need for protein. Some people thrive on a higher carbohydrate diet compared to protein and fats, while other thrive more on a higher protein diet in comparison to carbohydrates and fats.

No one really thrives on a high fat diet, unless you are an Eskimo maybe.

If you are a high protein person and are on a budget then your options are to either get a better job that pays more, or figure out how to get the most protein for your buck.

You do not have to listen to anything that I say but I am telling you that I look at protein as just protein.

Do you understand what I am saying here? Let me explain what I mean. When it comes to protein, the nutritional value that I get out of it is just protein. My body does not get its micronutrients from protein. Yours doesn't either, but people with **"certificates"** will tell you it does.

I also want my protein source with one exception to come with zero or next to zero fat. Especially if it is animal fat. Maybe many moons ago animal fat was good for us, but now our animals are pumped up with so many hormones that the fat is tainted and I try and avoid it as much as possible.

My one exception is Salmon and even that is tainted as our waters are polluted.

So how do we go about finding this happy medium when it comes to choosing the highest quality protein sources that we can afford?

Well the two cheapest and quality protein sources available without fat would be liquid egg whites (not substitute) and canned tuna in water. I know canned tuna isn't necessarily the best for us, but we are on a budget first of all, and second, we are not looking at protein as anything other than protein.

I hope that you can understand what I mean by this? I don't care what the paleo dipsticks and the Atkins dipsticks say, if you try and base your diet around protein as your main source of fuel, then you will not be as active and vibrant as if you based your diet around quality carbohydrates.

I am not saying that you should eat a 5 to 1 ratio of carbs to protein either. In fact I often eat about a 3.5 to 2 ratio myself, and when I feel that my body is telling me to do so, I eat an even ratio of carbs to protein. But the main point that I am making is that protein is not the same type of fuel for our bodies as is carbohydrates.

Believe me or not, I really don't care. I didn't pull this out of the thin air. This is just the way most peoples bodies are meant to run. Not everyone though, but most people are meant to run on carbs.

This is why I don't like all of those fads like Paleo and such. They take something that maybe 1% of the population can thrive on and try and force it down everyones throat and claim it as THE ONLY WAY to live.

This is ridiculous. Everyone that I have ever met that is a paleo bandwagon jumper eats freeze dried foods, drinks massive amounts of coffee, and thinks that it is the meat that is giving them life.

Our paleolithic ancestors didn't eat freeze dried foods and chug coffee like it was going out of style.

First of all take away their coffee and see how much life they have in them. The coffee is a replacement for glucose that the brain is desperately wanting. They are replacing sugar with a stimulant basically.

Coffee is a drug people.

It is just as addictive as crack and alcohol. I have known some coffee drinkers who I would consider them to be crack addicts. I bet to people who didn't know them personally, they probably appeared to be on crack to them.

I used to work with a very nice guy at a wind farm in Tehachapi California like 20 years ago. Wow! I cant believe it has been 20 years! I am only 37 but I have been working real jobs since I was 14.

I actually got to work on the very first of these really huge wind turbines that are everywhere now. But back then we were doing the first prototypes. The ones we were working on were called Z – 40's. Now I have drove through Tehachapi and the Mojave area and have seen that they have even bigger ones that even dwarf the Z – 40's.

We were slaves to that company. We did so much work and got so little credit for it. In fact that two year experience that I had with that company taught me a lot about business and how disgusting and ruthless it is.

I was just a kid, I wasn't even 18 yet, but I was an observant kid. A lot of the guys in the field hated my guts at first because they thought that I was some daddy's boy who got to go and play in the shop and get paid for doing nothing while they are up a hundred and fifty feet in the air in zero degree weather greasing old wind turbines.

I later earned some of those guys respect when they found out that I actually was a worker like they were. There were a few guys that really hated me still though. It was a jealousy thing, as they thought that I had the better job because I was in the shop and got to work on the **"top secret" Z - 40's** that they had been hearing about for years and weren't even allowed to go in the area where we were working on them. Or at least they thought they weren't.

You know how people are with classes. I try and treat everyone the same, but we were next to the suites who treated us like crap, but really treated the grease monkeys like they were lower than crap. So they always thought that we were like little spoiled sissy's who were brown nosers to the suites which we were not.

Well those few guys who still hated me ended up liking me in the end by the time that I got fired for tucking my pants into my boots! Hahahaha! I was kind of a rebel, and I hated their stupid rules like no tucking your pants into your boots, and no tying your coveralls around your waist. I got in trouble too many times for that kind of stuff and eventually gave my new boss a heart attack.

Or at least I like to say that I gave him one, because he had one not long after I was fired. One time I even got him to butt his nose up to mine and he tried to push me into a corner that was clear from all of the mirrors so the human resources people couldn't see.

Well I guess he didn't push me hard enough because the human resources lady seen the entire thing. I was laughing in his face as he was in my face telling me *"I did not get sent over here to be an FING baby sitter".*

He didn't really know me as he was new and had been transferred over from a different part of the area. He had just heard that I was really good at what I did (which I was) and was not used to having any kind of insubordination in his cult. Everyone who had worked under him was terrified of him. Even the guys who were no longer working under him all had fear of him.

I would laugh right in his face. Everyone thought that I was nuts. The guy took himself way too seriously. This is probably why he had a heart attack before he was even 40. People who think they are bad asses do not scare me one bit, unless they are gangbangers, in which those dumb kids will shoot a 90 year old grandma so they do scare the crap out of me.

I have learned over the years that those who seem to bark the loudest are the ones that bite the softest.

So to get me out of my new boss's hair, they decided to send me over to Texas, and to Vermont. They thought this might make me happy which it did as I wanted to be transferred into a field job which they wouldn't let me do. They wouldn't let me apply for a job that was considered lower than my title. But I was making less money than all those guys anyways???

So in Texas I volunteered for days to climb these 2 220 ft. anemometer and wind vane towers that no one wanted to climb. Everyone there was putting those things off and were about ready to literally draw straws to see who has to climb those things and assemble the lightning rod and anemometer and wind vane.

The weather was crazy there! There were lightning storms hourly most days. They would come through like a bat out of hell and we couldn't even go outside until they passed. We would have to watch out for them and try and time them out perfectly so that we could get our work done in between lightning storms.

So every day I kept eagerly raising my hand up like a 1st grader who knows the answer in class. I'll do it, I'll do it!

Finally, the guy who was in charge of me who also hated me at one point when I first started working there a couple of years before, but by this time I was his favorite person to work with and he requested me to be the person who wired the turbines up in the air with him while he was on the ground, had convinced the main guy in charge that I was able to climb those towers no problem and do the job.

Those two towers had no safety cable. And they had the girth of a person. I could wrap my arms around the tower and lock my fingers together. There were no pegs either to climb on.

The only way that I can explain it is the tower was like a tripod going straight up and connected together by galvanized steel pegs going up like in the letter Z. This is about as best as I can describe it. I am no rocket surgeon or anything so that's about as good as I can done do.

So I lanyard climbed these two things and had a blast doing so. I had to climb them with the lightning rod zip tied to my back and a 220 ft. rope attached to my harness which got pretty heavy by the time that I got to the top.

Then when I got myself all set up at the top and fastened into my little seat that I had to make with my lanyards I dropped my bucket down to pull up all of my tools. Well of course my partner wasn't going to let pull up a bucket without about ten lbs. of rocks inside of it? That would be rude of him.

It was funny to me though as I watched him run when I dumped out all those rocks from the heavens. Just kidding, I am not that stupid. Or am I?

I earned a lot of peoples respect that day as everyone was shaking at the knees when the thought of climbing those towers even came into their minds. They were even going to hire someone from Texas to climb those things for them.

At 37 would I still climb those things? I don't know, if they had a safety cable yes. But those pegs were about as thin as a number 2 pencil and that tower was very uncomfortable to climb. Those were some stupid towers that they must have bought at the lightning rod tower equivalent of the 99 cent store because they were not made very climber friendly.

At the very top with my weight up there it would rock and sway back and forth like 2 or 3 feet each side. It was pretty cool actually, and kind of spooky at the same time. It was a great experience for a stupid 18 year old kid. I am glad I did it.

So to get back to my coffee guzzling friend that I used to work with. Lets call him Larry (his real name is Larry). Well Larry was the definition of a workaholic if there truly is one. I personally do not consider a person to qualify as a workaholic unless they are working their fingers and minds to the bone in order to make someone else rich. People like me who work 25/8 for ourselves in order to make a better life and future for us and our families, I do not consider them to be workaholics.

This is just how I see things. Too many people complain about how hard they have to work when really they don't know how good they really have it (myself included). We all have it pretty good. We are well off enough to be reading this here on some type of an electronic device so we are pretty fortunate I think.

It was a regular thing for us to have to work 24 hours, 36 hours, even 48 hours straight with no sleep. We did this more times than anyone ever knew in order to get things finished by deadlines that were set that were impossible to meet.

Poor Larry was hardcore dedicated to that company and practically lived there. I am sure that by now he has gotten tossed out with the rest of the other hardcore people who thought that by now they would be sitting pretty, but those kinds of companies don't care about any of that stuff. I worked with some of those guys who dedicated their lives to that company for 20 – 30 years and got tossed out like yesterdays newspaper once they were of no use to them anymore.

If Larry continued his coffee abuse as he had been doing I am wondering if he is still even alive. I hope so because he was a very nice guy with a great work ethic. He was the kind of guy that would literally give a stranger the shirt off of his back if he needed to. He was the real deal.

This dude drank coffee like I drink water. And I drink about a gallon and a half of water a day. He had a coffee pot going in both break rooms. One was upstairs where the suites were and the other was down stairs were the rubes were. He was sort of a half a suite and was allowed upstairs but wasn't exactly wanted up stairs if you know what I mean.

I don't think that he had the proper college degree to earn the respect of all those suites. He was kind of a white trash kind of guy to them people.

I would go upstairs all the time and mess with the secretaries. All the girls upstairs liked me and I would get dirty looks from all the grumpy old CEO's and whatever else their stupid titles are, I really don't give two craps what title they are. People are people to me, and I will treat everyone with the same amount of respect. Until they disrespect me then it is on like donkey kong.

I even got a few of those suites to loosen their ties up and like me by the time it was all said and done. It took a while, but a few of those guys were actually ok if you just treat them like they are your equal and not like they are a God.

Most of those people don't like, and all of them don't respect brown nosers anyways.

Some celebrities are the same way as well. Not all celebrities, but I have met several celebrities in real life situations that I treated them just as if they were anyone else.

I remember meeting a pretty famous celebrity that most everyone would probably know who this person was if I said her name. We had a conversation long enough to introduce our names to each other which after she told me her name she followed it with do you know who I am?

I nonchalantly said oh yea I know who you are. I just don't worship celebrities. She was kind of floored but at the same time felt comfortable around me. I wasn't going to ask her for an autograph or talk about her job or anything like that.

So let me turn this ship back into the direction of protein before I go off on a rant about coffee that will probably turn everybody off to me completely. I feel a good rant brewing up and I have decided to catch myself in the act and will save it for another time and place.

Us people on a budget are going to have to implement protein sources from such things as canned tuna. But try and look at protein as just protein if you can. Your micronutrients come from your fruits and vegetable selections, and also I would recommend at least going with a pretty good multi vitamin if not doing what I do and kind of make up my own multi vitamin by purchasing only what I feel that my body needs separately.

Don't ever waste your money on a multi vitamin that is all in one tablet, or a gummy bear type of vitamin. You will just be wasting your time and more importantly money. So if you are going to look into multi vitamins, at least do some homework on them first as all multi vitamins are not created equally.

You get a decent amount of protein from complex carbohydrate sources such as oats, brown rice, lentils, and quinoa. All these I mentioned earlier in the carbohydrates section.

For some people this is plenty enough protein for their bodies needs. Not mine though, I need more protein in my body than from what I get in all of my carbohydrate sources.

I will show you an easy way how to figure out how many calories and how many grams of carbs, protein, and fats, that your body needs so that you can then divvy all that up and plan your meals out for the days to come.

Eating healthy on a budget is all about planning things out. You get the best bang for your buck if you know exactly what your body needs to run on high idle, and prepare ahead of time your meals daily. This is never ending and must become a routine that is imbedded into your system in order to succeed.

Protein is a tough one because I am so biased on the subject. I am trying to mix eating healthy with being on a budget here. I purposely did this so that I can get my two cents in as I would not be able to do it any other way.

So what I am saying here is at least try and keep your protein sources as close to no fat as possible. Stick to protein sources that are purely protein like canned tuna and liquid egg whites.

My only protein source that I want there to be fat along with it is salmon. I don't eat salmon everyday though, just as I do not eat canned tuna every day. I do drink liquid egg whites every single day.

Yes, I said I drink them. They are pasteurized so it is safe to drink liquid egg whites that you purchase at the store in a carton.

The majority of my protein comes from liquid egg whites. Do not confuse this with liquid egg white substitute.

I don't get too caught up in the whole which sources of protein are the most digestible, or the amino acid profiles of protein sources. I really don't even get caught up in which non animal sources of protein are complete proteins or not.

I used to be into all of that but I have lately just been going with what works for me and my body, and encourage everyone else to do the same. This is why I am constantly telling people to take even what I am saying with a grain of salt.

Take what 95% of people are saying and completely throw it in the trash. But open minded people who actually have been there and done that like myself, and not just tout verbiage they were taught in order to bring people into their cult. Take what we all say with a grain of salt, and sometimes throw in a shot of Tequila and a lime.

This does not mean that what anyone says wont work for you. But too many people rely on someone else to figure out their diets and food choices. Everybody has different needs and everyone should be in tune with their own bodies.

I don't eat cow, or pork. Cow, and pork can be cheap though. But you are getting the worst cuts of those animals with the worst fats going along with them.

Now if we are talking about wild animals, or grass fed animals such as buffalo, venison, and elk. That animal fat may not be quite so bad for you as would be the fat in cow or pork that you can easily buy at every grocery store in the nation.

But if you can afford to buy buffalo, venison, or elk, then you definitely would not be here reading this now would you?

So there might be something to my little method of keeping my protein sources clean from fats.

So if you are following my method, and lets say that you are a chicken person. Then you would be sticking to chicken breast only, instead of fatty chicken thighs, legs, and wings.

If you want to be a healthy individual your protein has got to be bland and boring.

Yes I said it...

You will never hear anyone tell you that. In fact everyone trying to sell you on a fad or a hyped up diet plan will tell you just the opposite of that. All the flavor is in the fat. People are addicted to fat, just as much as they are addicted to refined sugars, and some people even more so.

Like I said earlier, carbohydrates seems to be the red headed step child these days that gets the blame for everyone and their dogs fat problems. But has anyone ever stopped to think that maybe **FAT** might have just a little bit something to do with peoples fat problems?

Hmmmm I wonder...

It is all about balance. I believe that we were made to eat in a pretty balanced way. Each persons balance will vary individually, but I believe that balancing out protein, carbs, fat, and eating vegetables with your meals is what adds variety and flavor to our taste buds.

I don't care about taste buds. I have trained my taste buds to enjoy liquid egg whites and dried oats for crying out loud. I can grab a handful of oats and eat them just like that if I want to. I don't need flavor or condiments to be able to fuel my body with food. It is all just fuel to me, and I am not here to enjoy any of it. I have got better things to be doing with my life.

But not everyone is like this. In fact most people are not like this. Now I obviously enjoy my food don't get me wrong here. I love fruits of all kinds and the sweeter the better. I have just sponged out all of the cravings for refined sugars and over processed foods that in todays society are hard to avoid.

Many people are way too picky in my opinion. These are the type of people who are perfect candidates for rethinking their views on food, and to view it as fuel that their body needs to survive.

This will help these picky pallet people eat better.

At least consider my methods. Give them a try if you can. If you can avoid beef and pork and stick to chicken breast at the very least you will notice a big difference in how your body feels.

It will require baby steps for many people of course. But once a person learns how much protein their body needs a day. Then they learn how to divvy up that protein throughout their day, and figure out which percentages of that protein come from either complex carbs, or animal sources, they will notice a difference I can guarantee that. It may take a while to see it in the mirror, especially if a person spent 30 years going in the opposite direction. But people will notice a difference in how they feel inside which is really what counts in the whole grand scheme of things.

The bulk of your money budgeted for food is going towards protein. You may as well make it count and get the best sources of protein that your money can buy. Especially if you are trying to feed an entire family.

Fats:

People are stupid when it comes to fat sources. I have known people who think that they are on the ball with their calories and so forth. They believe that they have every single macronutrient figured out that goes into their body, and for the most part they do.

But there are two macronutrient sources that many people have a hard time figuring out how to count and one of them is fats. The other one is alcohol. Most people don't even know that alcohol is a macronutrient.

Now days people are sort of aware of good fats, and bad fats and all that good stuff that goes along with it. But everyone is only basing their views on which fats are good or bad depending on who told it to them.

There are people out there who confuse and lump in saturated fat with hydrogenated fat. Our bodies need saturated fat, our bodies reject hydrogenated fat. But there are many people out there who will be saturated fat conscious because they were told by someone that saturated fat was bad for them, all while not being hydrogenated fat conscious and eating foods daily that are cooked in those types of oils that contain hydrogenated fat.

No one is really educated on anything when it comes to foods. Everything is just hearsay anymore. Especially in the cyber world where anyone can put something up on the web and people will view it as fact. Don't ever believe anything that you read on the internet ok. Don't even believe me. Figure things out for yourself, then go out and find which people that you feel have also figured things out for themselves and surround yourself with those types of people.

One thing that is so great about being on a strict budget is that you are pretty much forced to have to cook your own food. I know that this may seem like a chore to many people but this is actually a blessing in disguise.

To eat right you have got to know your carb sources. High glycemic and low glycemic. Everything that I mentioned above is low glycemic carbs. Even the fruit that I mentioned. But high glycemic fruit is fine, like raisins, and grapes and prunes and whatever else would be considered high glycemic. All this stuff is fructose though.

The high glycemic carbs to stay away from all will come from processed food sources. Eat whatever fruit you desire.

The same thing goes for protein. Know your protein sources and know what is riding along with it.

The same rule applies when it comes to fats.

See if we separate all three of these macronutrients then we can get a better understanding of what is in them first of all, and also how much of what our bodies need to get through our day.

You don't need to cook your food in anything!

Remember to eat healthy we want *BORING FOOD.* The majority of people who cook their own foods problems lie in the oils they cook them in.

So many people are so close to eating fairly healthy, but they cook their foods in bad oils, or they use too much of good oils, or they overheat the wrong types of oils that are not meant to go over a certain temperature like olive oil.

Coconut oil seems to be the latest and greatest cure of the 21st century since…?

…????

…???

…???

Sorry I am still trying to think of an ending for this. I don't even have one, this is how dumb I think these coconut oil cure people are.

I was raised on coconut oil since I was born. Way before anyone ever decided to make it a slippery bandwagon for gullible people to jump onto.

I love coconut oil, and I eat it almost every single day by the teaspoon. So I am not knocking it. And coconut oil actually did cure my mom of something I swear to God. She cured herself of a skin disorder that not one **QUACK** that she went to could figure out what it was, nor did they really care to.

They prescribed her steroids and creams that made it worse. One of them even went so far as to try and tell her that it was all in her head and wanted to prescribe her antidepressants. Those **QUACKS** get a big old bulbous hairy knuckled middle finger from me for the things that they put her through trying to use her as a lab rat.

She works in the health department for a government job where she deals with blood all day. I guarantee she contracted whatever skin disease she had from there.

Anyways to make a long story short. The skin disease looked as if her legs had been burnt very badly. They tried to tell her it was shingles and all kinds of other things that it most definitely was not. And it definitely wasn't all in her head like that dumb BRAWD told her it was.

She was pretty much bed ridden for three years at least, maybe even more as this was several years ago and I forget how long she was out of commission for. But she couldn't do anything other than apply coconut oil onto her body all day and all night long for at least three years straight. It was brutal to watch.

We would order coconut oil 30 – 40 gallons at a time no kidding. It was worse from her knees down but it was pretty much on her entire body and would move around and attack certain areas.

She basically had to live like a basted turkey on thanksgiving or her body especially her legs would turn into the Sahara desert. I do not wish this on anyone, not even the **QUACK** who told her it was all in her head.

So coconut oil did save her life in a way as she was forced to just self medicate by constantly staying in a lather of coconut oil 24/7/365/3, at least three years. She still needs to apply coconut oil to her legs even to this day as this is still inside of her body.

So as much as I believe in coconut oil even my mom would have to say that these people have taken it and turned it into another fad for people to hop on and eventually hop off as their eyes get attracted to whatever the new shiny object is that will be placed in front of their faces, and miss all of the real benefits that coconut oil has to offer.

All of the vegetable oils have many great benefits to them. They can do great things inside and outside of the body.

We get a decent amount of fat in our carbohydrate sources that just go along for the ride. Most people don't think about the fat that is in foods such as rice, oats, and even a little bit of fat in fruits. Avacado is a fruit and it is mostly fat. If you are eating the right amount of calories that are coming from the right sources you can easily get 15 – 30 grams of fat depending on what you eat all from carbohydrate sources that go along for the free ride.

Some peoples bodies may only need 30 grams of fat. I know that I need more than that so I use fat as a supplement that I eat with my foods.

We are on a budget, but this does not mean that we should just buy the cheapest fat sources possible.

In fact, out of the three main macronutrient sources I would suggest that the fat source might even be the most crucial, at least if optimum health is the main focus.

Fat makes us fat. So does refined sugars and over processed foods. But even good fats can make us and keep us fat if we are consuming too much of it.

I have discovered over the years that if I keep my fat sources down to just a few I can easily regulate and keep track of how much fat I am eating a day by way of grams.

So my personal fat sources outside of what I get from other foods are:

Salmon or Krill oil

Coconut oil (extra virgin if affordable)

Canned olives

So these are basically my three main fat sources that I choose to eat. I switch things up from time to time like I will occasionally buy a bottle of olive oil or grape seed oil. But I pretty much just stick to these three because I just feel like doing so. It works for me. I am not telling anyone to follow exactly what I do, I am just throwing these ideas out there so that people can get a good baseline to work from.

Canned olives are cheap where I live and I like to use them in my salads for filler. They are high in fat. I know that canned foods are not the best, and I do not consider any canned foods to be part of my micronutrient intake for the day, but I am on a budget so I need to work within the boundaries of what I can afford.

I would much rather spend more money on krill oil, or coconut oil, so I try and penny pinch in other areas so that I can do so.

I eat very good for being so poor. I am actually kind of proud of myself for the way that I am able to juggle around my budget in order to eat the way that I do. I would rather eat healthy foods then have a roof over my head, if this is any indication of how highly I prioritize my fuel for my body.

A little later I will show you how to figure out your macro's so that you are not getting too much of one and not enough of another.

If you are going to go with oils for your fats, I would recommend oils such as olive oil, and grape seed oil, and even peanut oil. All these oils are not cheap but they are fairly easy to find in most grocery stores. I would also recommend going for the highest quality possible.

This is why I do the fish oil as well. Not just for the omega 3 benefits but I also like to have a little bit of animal fat from fish. Krill oil is my fish oil of choice but it is very expensive. So I like to occasionally buy Krill oil in between Salmon oil which I buy all that online. I am not an affiliate of this company although I wish I were, but I buy all of my fish oil from swansonhealth.com. There are so many brands to choose from, expensive to affordable. I go with what my budget allows me to purchase at that very moment.

I actually order my coconut oil from that same company as well. I am always looking for sales and they will sometimes have great deals on bulk purchasing.

Another great company which I am also not affiliated with is tropicaltraditions.com. They sell coconut oil by the 5 gallon buckets. My mom actually discovered this company when she was going through her ordeal. They are a bit pricey, but they have some of the highest quality coconut oil out there.

I am a pretty high carb person and even I don't get enough fats from my carb sources. So I would recommend that everyone at least pick one fat source for your daily intake. Even if it is only a can of olives a day. It is not the best source of fat, but it is definitely not the worst, or even close to the worst.

You would be better off not eating any fat source other than what is in your carbs then to buy cheap oils made with hydrogenated fats.

I know you paleo people are staring daggers at me right now I can sense this. You are all ready to spear me and eat me alive right now because I have not yet mentioned the latest and greatest fad that you all have been taught to be the greatest invention since freeze dried fruits known as almond butter.

Almond butter is great. Nutritionally, it is the equivalent to peanut butter though which is also great.

What was that?

Oh you don't believe me?

Oh I am lying about that?

Ok...

Who told you almond butter was superior to peanut butter?

Oh your "nutritional coach/?/?/?/?/?/?/?/?/?/?"

Ok well you all keep listening to them then and have a great day.

For the rest of you people who are not narrow minded, almond butter is great. So is peanut butter, cashew butter, sun flower seed butter, and coconut butter if they are in their natural form.

So pretty much any kind of butter that wont die and go rotten if you put it in your cupboard don't eat.

Natural almond butter and peanut butter are great sources of affordable fat, and also have a decent little amount of carbs and protein to go along with it.

The only problem that I have with those types of butters is what tends to go along with them like jelly's and breads. Most people who eat peanut butter or almond butter do not do so with a spoon. I know that I love a spoonful of natural peanut butter, but most people do not eat like that. So most people will be making PB&J SAMICH'S and ruining their overall health in the process. Not that the occasional PB&J aren't ok, it is just not something that I would want to make a habit of, especially if you are not a young active kid. Many people on a budget will begin to use PB&J's as their main staple. I know how people think. They are easy to make and taste delicious. It would be no problem for someone to be able to go through an entire loaf of bread a day if this was their staple food.

If you are wanting to use one of these types of butters as your fat source, then I will give you some of my favorite smoothie recipes in a little bit taken from a couple of my smoothie recipe books so that you don't have to get lured into the PB&J trap.

Condiments:

Most condiments are bad for us.

Let me just get that out of the way. But this does not mean that we are not going to have a condiment here and there, as long as it does not become a habit that we must have in order to be able to eat our foods.

Some people need to go cold turkey off of condiments. This sucks I know, but that may be the only way for many people. I am not a condiment guy so having no condiments on my foods is no big deal to me. I do use a few condiments that I can do without if need be.

Not all condiments are bad for us like such things as cinnamon, or 100% stevia, or even sea salt isn't bad for us no matter what those dumb diet fad pushers tell you about sodium. Too much of anything is bad for us, and I can go on a long rant about sodium and how it has nothing to do with fat gain but I wont.

Sodium can play a role in water retention. Water retention and fat storage are two completely different things. This is one of the reasons I say throw away the scale. I will not allow myself to rant about this subject here, but I will somewhere else as this whole sodium is the enemy and cause for fat gain thing drives me up the wall. But hey, I am no Donald duck waddling quack, or an internet "nutritionist" who won my certificate in a fitness enthusiast contest to see who was the most enthusiastic about fitness!!!!!!!!!!!!!!!!!!

I am over enthused!!!!!!!!!!!!!!!!!!

If your concerned with overall health and not just trying to eat the cheapest way possible, then pick and choose your condiments wisely. Most condiments are the feces of food (if they can even be called food). It is sad but I have seen many people who eat more condiments than they do food.

I cant tell you what to buy, but I can tell you what condiments that I allow myself to eat. I would also say to steer clear of most liquids and oily condiments like mayonnaise and dressings.

I eat Franks red hot sauce occasionally when I want to spice up my rice. The worst ingredient in there is the salt, which I am sure doesn't come from a good source but I eat so little of it that this really doesn't concern me much.

If you are a hot sauce person like myself, then read the ingredients of the bottles and try and find the one with the least amount of ingredients. There are a few with only a few ingredients in them like Franks. They generally will have the pepper, vinegar, water, salt, and maybe some garlic. Anything other than that would probably be some kind of food coloring or a preservative. I would stay away from those as much as possible.

If health is your priority here, then you absolutely must stay away from things such as mayonnaise, and dressings. For many people this is where it gets tough for them. I have known a lot of people who have thought that they were switching their diet over to a more healthy lifestyle and eating more fruits and vegetables which they are doing just that. But when I see how they go about eating their fruits, and especially vegetables, they are just basically smothering them with condiments in order to get through the feeding and force down some veggies. This will not last long for these kinds of people as they are just trying to mask the root of the problem.

Some good condiments are things such as 100% stevia, and cinnamon. I use both of these things in my oats in the morning. For people who are addicted to refined sugar, this is a great combination to cut the refined sugar cold turkey.

Real stevia is for some reason expensive these days and not always easy to find, so always read the label and look for 100% stevia. You don't want any other ingredients. A stevia and cinnamon combo not only tastes sweet enough for those with a sweet tooth, but cinnamon does help regulate blood sugar.

I always prepare my morning meal the night before, and inside of my oats I always dump in about 5 grams of cinnamon powder along with a few sprinkles of 100% stevia.

Calorie counting and macros:

I think about 5 or 6 people have read my book How to Count Calories Correctly! Hahaha, that's ok, at that time when I wrote it along with some other books I had absolutely no clue about SEO's and keywords and just how important they are in getting your book in front of peoples eyeballs online to see.

I am not a professional online marketing weasel thank God, so I was just writing on subjects that I felt like writing on. I still do that by the way, I have just since learned a little bit on how to keyword my book titles and a few other things in order to get them at least to the middle of the line. This is such a crazy business behind the scenes. I could tell you so many things about this business that would not only shock you, but possibly drive you away from ever wanting to read another book again.

A part of me is sort of glad that not many people have bought that book because I am not so sure that many people would get what I was trying to imply there.

Counting calories is easy to do but at the same time most people do it wrong. Not only that, but most people don't need to really even be worrying about the actual number of calories that they eat. What they should be worrying about is the sources in which those calories come from.

I don't like to teach people who are desperate how to count calories. This is because they are wanting to do so only so that they can keep them as low as possible.

I want to teach people to count calories so that they can make sure that they are fueling their bodies with enough calories to get them through their day, not keep them below a certain number that they read on the internet or some dillwad told them to eat in order to lose weight.

As important as the Basal Metabolic Rate is, and it is important to know at the very least to have a nice starting point.

It still wont do us any good knowing our BMR if we don't select the right ratio's of macronutrients that our bodies individually needs to fit inside of those caloric boundaries that we are assigning ourselves, all based on a theory that we are going to burn X amount of calories a day every day the same way day in and day out.

I don't know about you, but I live in the real world.

The real world does not care about theories, or even science. I am someone who no longer even believes in studies as I have found them to always come from biased sources. You can easily find two different studies on the same topic, both claiming that the exact opposite of the other one is the superior way to go about doing fill in the blank.

I just worry about my own body, and what makes me run on high idle, and what keeps me healthy. And I encourage others to do the same thing.

The Basal Metabolic Rate is good to know but it is not accurate for everyone, and it is also just a platform to start from. Many of the better nutritionists will use the BMR as their base and then add in a few hundred or so calories depending on the persons activity level into their daily intake. They let that marinade for a while and then start to make adjustments according to how the persons body reacts to those specific number of calories.

This is all good, but there is so much more to it than just simply adding in and taking away calories.

I have got a little saying that I actually first wrote in a song lyric of mine but I also use it when I talk about this health and fitness industry. I say if they can confuse you, then they can use you.

These self proclaimed nutritional experts just want to keep people confused and dumb so that they rely on their guidance and council for the rest of their lives.

Figuring out your calories and macros is super easy. Coming up with a plan and sticking to it is the hard part that requires mental toughness.

Everyone first needs a platform to stand on.

It may not be the best platform to stand on, but at least for the time being the closest platform to use as your reference point from where to begin building your caloric structure is the platform that you are already standing on.

If you are currently eating ding dongs, doughnuts, fast foods, and all of the other processed junk foods that people eat in todays world then the best way to go about changing it is to confront it head on.

I am super picky about who I help one on one, as I do not just go around trying to generate massive amounts of clients in order to get filthy rich off of these people who don't have a clue about what they are doing when it comes to nutrition.

I do enjoy helping people though. And when I do I only do so if I feel that their mind is ready for it. Otherwise they would just be wasting their time and money.

The very first thing that I always tell people is to not change anything about the way that they are eating.

Yet...

I want people to learn how to count their macros first from what they are currently eating now, not what they will soon be eating or attempting to eat later in order to turn the ship around in the other direction towards optimum health.

It sounds so simple, but most of these experts do not do this with their clients. That is because I live in the real world with everyone else. All of these experts seem to live in some fantasy world where they have delusions of grandeur and believe that they hover above their clients.

If I am searching for a nutritional advisor the first thing that I am going to ask them is if I can please go to their house and rummage through their refrigerator and pantry. If they are too far away for me to do that then I would ask them to please send me as many pictures as possible of what is inside of their kitchen right now, and what it is that they put into their mouth to utilize as fuel daily.

Then I would ask them to explain to me why they eat the way that they do. If there is anything in their refrigerator that would be considered "junk" foods I would want them to explain to me why those are in there and how often they eat those types of foods.

The first meeting with a "nutritional expert" of any kind should be the client bombarding them with personal questions pertaining to the experts diet and why they eat the way that they do.

Try it and see how far you get.

No one eats perfect. These high and mighty nutritionist's want you to think they do, but in all reality they probably eat just as bad as their clients if not worse. If someone was born with the genetics to be obese, they will be obese. If someone was born with the genetics to walk around under 12% body fat, they will walk around with under 12% body fat for the most part.

If I were to bring someone over to look at my fridge right now at this very moment I would have a bottle of Franks Red Hot Sauce, a container of pepperoncini's, a little container of relish, a six pack of Sam Adams, and a few Becks light beers that would be considered "bad" fuel for my body. If this were last week I would also have a loaf of whole wheat bread in my fridge.

I could easily explain why I have those in my refrigerator, and also why and when I choose to eat and drink those things.

I am not trying to put any of those people down, I just wish that they would start living the life that they get paid big bucks to tell others to live. On second thought, I am trying to put them down who am I kidding here.

Even these holier than thou raw vegan people do not eat 100% raw all the time. The poor people who worship the ground that they walk on are being bamboozled into thinking that these people are above being human. You also would have to be a rich son of a gun to eat the way that they tell their flock of sheep that they should eat anyways. Many people who try and live that lifestyle and cant end up feeling that they are not worthy of it and just give up completely. I am not a vegan, but I have seen people try to go completely vegan at the drop of a dime because they were moved or touched in some way to do so. Only to soon find out that they either cant afford it, or they feel as if they cant live up to the standard that was set by people who do not live up to that very same standard themselves.

This is the way of the world. There are people who talk it, and there are people who walk it. And sometimes there are people who walk it and talk it.

There is no better place to begin your calorie counting than to begin with the crap that you are already putting into your body. Now you will have something to compare to later down the road when you are feeding yourself with the best sources of fuel that you possibly can.

It is hard to keep an accurate amount of calories when we are eating things such as fast foods and packaged foods. This is a good thing. It will make the person who is dedicated to eating better work harder in the beginning trying to keep track of all their calories from all the different sources in which they get them from.

A dedicated person will want to start eliminating many of their calorie sources once they see for themselves just how useless many of them are.

Calories come from these four sources:

Alcohol

Fats

Protein

Carbohydrates

There are 7 calories per gram of alcohol.

9 calories per gram of fat.

4 calories per gram of protein.

4 calories per gram of carbohydrates.

This is really easy stuff to remember, and even easier once a person gets their staples down to what they want to use for fuel in their bodies. We are not bodybuilders competing in our little pink thong bikinis on stage so there is no need for us real humans to be weighing our foods.

This is another thing that makes me laugh when nutritional experts have their clients weighing their foods. This is freaking stupid. Unless you plan on getting on stage all greased up and roided out of your mind in a pink thong then there is no need to weigh any of your food.

Throw away both the food scale and the scale that you stand on every single morning and start basing your caloric intake on how you feel first, and second how you look in a mirror completely naked if aesthetics are your thing.

If you are going to weigh your food, make sure that you are weighing your food so that you are getting in enough calories not so that you can keep them as low as possible.

The tough part for most people is trying to figure out their macros throughout the day and the many different sources in which these macros come from.

If you eat lots of fast foods then you have got to figure out how much fat, protein, and carbs are in whatever it is that you shove down your pie hole. This often requires a person to have to get on their computer and google this stuff. It takes time and effort which is what we want. The longer it takes someone to initially try and figure out all of their macros that they are currently eating, the more motivating it is to them to try and eliminate all of the unnecessary foods that they eat. Eventually you get to where you can just eyeball everything and pretty much know exactly what you are eating both calories and macros wise.

Condiments are tough for people to keep track of as well. I have known many people who are pretty good at keeping track of their main sources of foods. But easily forget about all of the condiments that they eat those foods with. Some people can easily eat more than 500 calories just in condiments alone. Some people even a lot more than that. So you have got to count all of your condiment macros as well.

Then it is all about keeping a good logging of everything that you eat. Each person is different depending on their drive and dedication to this, but for someone who is dedicated to start eating healthier a solid couple of weeks worth of logging down every single thing that they have eaten without consciously changing their diet should be enough for them to have something to look back on and try and start figuring out how many calories their body needs to run on, and also what types of foods it is that they need to eliminate from their meal rolodex.

This is obviously the very short version of this process, and I am going to try and simplify it as best as I can here in this short chapter, but basically before you start to break your food down into actual meals if that is what you choose to do, you will first need to break down which percentages of macros fits into to the overall calorie number that you are going to begin your journey with.

There are so many fat people who are under caloried and malnourished.

I know this is hard to believe but this is so true. Forget what you have heard about calories. All these theories floating around about calories in calories out are nothing but filler designed to tickle your ears and impress you. Their job is to convince you into believing that whoever is telling you all of this new scientific sounding stuff is smart.

An obese person has a better chance of living healthier and losing **FAT** weight and keeping it off on a diet of 3000+ calories coming from the proper sources than they do on a diet consisting of half of those calories.

Can they lose weight on 1,500 calories? Yes of course, mostly water weight. They will also be mal nourished and weaker than a 2 year old baby.

It all depends on how much fat a person has got to lose as well as how long they have spent building that fat onto their body. Each individual will be different, but the one thing that is consistent is that over time a calorie reduced diet plan is not ever sustainable.

EVER!

Neither do any of those fasting type of diets whether they are water, juice, or intermittent. They all just damage the metabolism.

When the body thinks it is being deprived of nutrients it will hold onto the fat as a survival mechanism. For those people who are obsessed with the scale and seeing a specific weight on it. **Muscle outweighs fat**. So if the body is losing muscle and water along with some fat too, these people all think that they are doing something good because they see that weight drop on the scale. And they are doing something good, but they are just not going about the right way of doing it.

It amazes me how people can take 30 years to fatten up, and then turn around and want to slim down in less than 30 days.

The body does not work this way. You can lose 30 lbs. in 30 days, or 100 lbs. in 100 days, or whatever the hook is that these people are trying to lure overweight people in with. But most of that weight is going to be water weight.

If a person has got a lot of body fat to lose, then some of the fat will shed along with muscle and water. But once the initial fat is shed and the fat begins to turn into **"stubborn fat",** the body will now hold onto this fat as a survival mechanism.

Each person has a different point where the fat will become stubborn and not want to shed from the body. For a person who has never been more than 12% body fat, some of them can even have stubborn body fat begin at 12 or 11% as they are already at a pretty low percentage anyways.

Someone who has never been under 30% in their entire life can face the same situation in where their body has become used to this body fat percentage and it will become stubborn at 30%.

Some people are 35% body fat but they can easily get down to 20%, and this is where the fat starts to become stubborn. Some people can float around from 5% to 12% fairly easily. But these people usually are on anabolic steroid cycles year round. Someone who is naturally around 12% body fat will hit a wall at some point and the fat will become stubborn once they get around 9 or 8% unless they are cycling cutting steroids. This is just the way it is. I am not saying that you cant pass that wall without some extra help, I am just saying that everyone will hit a wall at some point and each person will hit that wall at different points in their fat loss.

The point that I am trying to make here, is that everyone who puts themselves on a calorie restricting diet will at some point hit a wall in their very near future if they continue down the road of calorie restriction. They will also damage their metabolism and take several steps backwards in overall health and long term weight management in order to lose X amount of lbs. on a scale, or lose X amount of inches on their waist line.

People need to calorie up from the right sources and be as active as possible. I do not understand the calorie restricting mindset these days.

So lets fast forward through all of the trial and error and screwing up your calorie logs over and over again, and lets say that you finally figured it all out and kept a half way decent log of what foods that you have been eating for the last couple of weeks or so.

So now you would need to start comparing the total calories that you consumed from each day to the next. So lets say Monday you ate a total of 2,300 calories roughly, and Tuesday you ate a total of 1,600 calories roughly, and Wednesday you ate a total of 2,100 calories roughly, and Thursday you ate a total of 1,500 calories roughly, and Friday, Saturday, and Sunday you ate 3,000+ calories on each of those days, and so on and so on.

Most people will see differences in their daily caloric intake like this. Not everyone of course, but a lot of people eat small all week and then bigger on the weekends. This isn't always bad, but depending on the persons metabolism it isn't always a good thing either.

But this is still a good place to start from. You now can add up all of the calories for the week and divide them by the number of days to figure out your average daily caloric intake.

Both males and females can use this same method, but for example I will use a 200 lb. male. If you are a 140 lb. male or female use the same method per whatever your body weight is. Do not do what most people do with this method and use the weight that YOU WISH YOU WERE. This is a huge mistake that people make. They are trying to put the cart before the horse. If you are 250 lbs. and would like to eventually be 150 lbs. it will take time and patience to get there, but if this is a realistic weight for a person than they can get there and stay there if they go about doing things the correct way. I talk about how to do this in other books, and I may just write one small book dedicated only to this one subject in the near future. But for this book I am just going to lay out the simple version of how to go about creating a good platform to stand on. This is a good solid base in which to start from.

So lets use a 200 lb. male who is 20% body fat as our example. Lets say that he instinctively eats around 2,500 calories a day on average and remain around 200 lbs. and 20% body fat.

Now our guy has got all kinds of things to take into account here. First he needs to ask himself if he is happy with the way that he feels? Does he feel vibrant and as healthy as a race horse at 20% body fat? The honest answer is no.

I am not talking about trying to look all ripped and chiseled up in the mirror. This means nothing to the average person. You can go on some good anabolic cycles and go from 20% body fat to 7% with muscles that you never even knew existed in just a short 6 month period if you do it right. I am saying to ask yourself if you feel like a thoroughbred race horse where you stand at that very moment?

So now our guy here needs to begin to figure out his macros. Where exactly are those 2,500 calories coming from? What percentage of those calories are coming from either fat, protein, carbs, or alcohol?

So after figuring out where all of the calories are coming from lets just throw up some easy numbers out there and say that he figured out that his average daily macros looks something like this:

Fat: 150 grams X 9 calories per gram = 1,350 calories from fat.

Protein: 150 grams X 4 calories per gram = 600 calories from protein.

Carbs: 150 grams X 4 calories per gram = 600 calories from carbs.

He doesnt drink alcohol so he is getting zero calories from that. Also as far as carbs goes just count them all the same in the beginning. Don't worry about high glycemic vs. low glycemic, fibrous vs. refined sugar vs. fructose, and all that stuff just yet. A carb is not just a carb, but when a person is first beginning to learn how to figure out their macros the last thing they need is another distraction that would only confuse them and slow down their progress.

So this comes out to a total of 2,550 calories which is close enough to the 2,500 that I said earlier. We will just round it down to 2,500 calories. More than likely a person who is new to this will be way off on their calorie counting anyways.

So without ever seeing this individual and what he looks like while at 20% body fat, and eating roughly around 2,500 calories a day to remain looking the same. I would say that he lives a pretty sedated lifestyle.

2,500 calories is pretty low for a 200 lb. man. That is also a ridiculous amount of fat grams in comparison to the protein and carbs. Good thing for him that he doesn't drink. If he did he wouldn't be consuming 2,500 calories I can promise you that.

So percentage wise this guys macros looks like this:

Fat: 53%

Protein: 23.5%

Carbs: 23.5%

This is a pretty typical diet percentage wise when it comes to macros. Many people get around half if not more of their calories coming from fat. An alcoholics chart would look a lot different than that and they would obviously have an entirely different set of problems to go along with it. But for all of the people who say that it is only about calories in vs calories out, the human body will show it to be otherwise.

You can easily be 20% body fat while consuming 2,500 calories a day, easy. You can be 20% body fat while consuming 1,500 calories a day. You can be 10% body fat while consuming 4,000 calories a day as well. It all depends on the persons metabolism and how active they want to be, and how dedicated they are to making those calories come from the absolute best sources available.

So now our 200 lb. guy is going to have to give himself some realistic goals to aim for. Goals that he can achieve, not just some unrealistic goals of dropping a bunch of fat and getting an 8 pack overnight. It will not happen this way. You cant get down to 7% body fat and below without first getting down below 20%. Some peoples bodies will simply never allow them to get down to 7% body fat naturally. In fact most peoples bodies wont allow them to get down that low naturally without some major side effects.

If you want Winstrol thin skin, then do Winstrol like everyone else does, on top of many other types of gear.

So the hard part for our guy here is going to be figuring out which calorie percentages he needs for his body to start to run on a higher fat burning idle than it is currently. And I will say this, 50%+ calories coming from fat is not going to cut the mustard.

But he will not be able to jump down to 10% or so overnight. He will have to gradually wean himself off of the fat overtime. This is tough because many people are more addicted to fat than they think. Refined sugars gets a bad rap these days as they probably should, but they should not get all of the blame for fat gain. A calorie is not a calorie, and the body does not metabolize all calories the same. Fat slows down the metabolizing of the fuel that you put into your mouth. Sugar speeds it up. Yes, even refined sugar speeds it up. Actually, refined sugar speeds it up even more as it does not contain fiber that also slows down the digestion of foods that carb sources contains.

Fat = slow

Sugar = fast

Remember I am not a Donald duck waddling quack with a stethoscope around my neck. So please do not ever listen to a single word that comes out of my mouth or fingers.

But even a moron like myself knows that too much fat makes you slow and fat. Just like too much sugar makes you hyper and bouncing off the walls like a crack head. Whoever came up with all of these high fat diets for weight loss in my opinion were all high on something themselves.

But the dumb people of the world eat this stuff up!

So for now our guy is going to leave his total daily calories at around 2,500. If he wants to get active he will need to up those calories based on how active it is that he wants to be. But for the time being he will just want to stay around 2,500 calories.

He obviously lives a pretty sedated life, and does not have a job where he needs to expend a great amount of energy. People should always take into account their jobs when it comes to figuring out how many calories they expend each day. I have worked in a tough trade of Masonry for 15 years of my life where it also stays over 100 degrees in the summer where I live. So I know a little something about expending massive amounts of calories a day slaving away for some arrogant prick who considers you to be nothing more than an assembly line with a heartbeat.

Anyone who works a job like that is doing more damage to their bodies than good, no matter how many calories they consume a day.

Many of these people rely on drugs (legal and illegal) and alcohol in order to get them through their day.

So the easiest and fastest way for our guy to figure out how he is going to change the macro percentages in his diet and slowly start to eliminate all of the garbage that he is currently putting into his body is this.

Just simply take the body weight that he is currently at which is 200 lbs. and that will be his **protein in grams** that will be consumed daily. So a 200 lb. man will eat 200 grams of protein which amounts to 800 calories. 800 calories divided by 2,500 total calories comes out to 32% of his total calories are now going to come from protein.

Now as far as carbs goes, right now forget about the glycemic index, and sugary vs. fibrous carbs and all of that and just focus on total carbs. just take the 200 lbs. of body weight and eat 1.5 grams of carbs per pound of body weight. So 200 lbs. X 1.5 grams = 300 carbs. This equals out to 1,200 calories. 1,200 calories coming from carbs divided by 2,500 total calories comes out to be 48% of calories now are going to be coming from carbs.

Now that 48% of calories coming from carbs plus the 32% calories coming from protein equals out to be 80% of calories in total so far. This leaves 20% left over for the fat calories to come from. See how we have completely flipped this guys eating style around so that now he is burning fuel from carbs rather than fat.

Eventually I would say to get that fat even lower closer to 10%, but many people don't want to be lean. They are happy and even feel better at around 20% of their total calories coming from fat. This is completely fine as long as that is what they desire.

So 2,500 total calories minus 1,200 calories from carbs, and minus 800 calories from protein, leaves him with a total of around 500 calories that are going to be coming from his fat sources.

500 calories divided by 9 calories per gram of fat leaves us with around 55.5 grams of fat a day that our 200 lb. guy is going to be consuming. So essentially he upped his protein just a little bit, and doubled his carbs, and cut his fat down by around 100 grams. Once the carb sources and the fat sources start to come from clean non processed foods, after some time for the body to get used to this new way of fueling it, this dude will begin to run like a well oiled machine.

This right here is the basic platform that many **MEN AND WOMEN** both can benefit from.

Protein: 1 gram per pound of bodyweight.

Carbs: 1.5 grams per pound of body weight.

Fat: Fill in the blanks once you figure out your total caloric intake per what your body is telling you.

IT GETS NO EASIER THAN THIS FOLKS.

Now from this platform it is easy to start to make adjustments here and there as your body is telling you to do so. A person must also learn how to listen to their own body throughout all of this and continue to do so for the rest of their life.

For me personally a good percentage that I like to use to stay lean and strong at the same time is:

70% carbs

25% protein

5% fat

All while still keeping my protein at around 1 gram per pound of body weight and sometimes even higher. 25% total calories coming from protein does not mean that I don't get in my fair share of protein. I just eat the right foods in order to do so. This is why I tell people to start with their protein and work their way out from there. If someone does

this correctly this will limit them to only certain types of foods that they can eat in order to fit into their macros correctly.

I feel good at around these percentages as far as my macros goes, especially during our boiling hot summers where I live. Climate has got a lot to do with macro percentages also. As the weather gets colder, I will naturally start to lower my carbs a bit and add a little more fat into my diet. I don't even really know why I do this, but I do know that I do and I just go with what my body is telling me to do.

So in the summer I might be 70/25/5, and by the middle of winter I might be 60/25/15. Give or take a few percentages depending on my bodies needs.

Both men and women can utilize this type of eating style. This is not just for men, nor is it just for people who are trying to get big, ripped, swole, or what have you. It is for anyone and everyone who wants to feel at their best.

I am making all of this sound a whole lot easier than it really is of course, but once people get used to it, it really does become super easy. In the beginning it is a chore, I am not going to lie about that. But after some time and getting used to knowing exactly what goes into your body and why it goes in there, all this stuff becomes **EYEBALLABLE** if that is even a word.

You will be able to just eyeball everything and be within just a few calories every single time.

So our 200 lb. man now will be spending his next six months to a year trying to clean up his food choices hopefully, and also keep figuring out where his total daily calories should be roughly. I personally think that 2,500 calories for a 200 lb. young man is low. But each person will ultimately be the decider in how much of, and what it is they are going to be eating.

A person who is motivated enough to go this far in their calorie counting, usually is also motivated enough to get on some type of exercise schedule as well. So 2,500 calories would definitely not be sufficient enough to keep this guy running on a full tank.

This is the very short version and pretty much the platform to stand on when it comes to macros and calorie counting. I hope that it made sense for you who are reading this.

Just remember that the ultimate goal is to eliminate processed foods. The rest of the pieces seem to fall into place easier once that one thing is accomplished.

It is not so much just about the overall calorie number, rather it is more about where those calories are coming from.

If you want to lose fat, flip those macro percentages upside down and let the body begin to start to run on its preferred choice of fuel which is **NON PROCESSED** carbohydrates.

These are the absolute basics of all basics right here. And even by following just these simple basics and nothing more, people can start to feel a difference in how they feel, and eventually over time how they look.

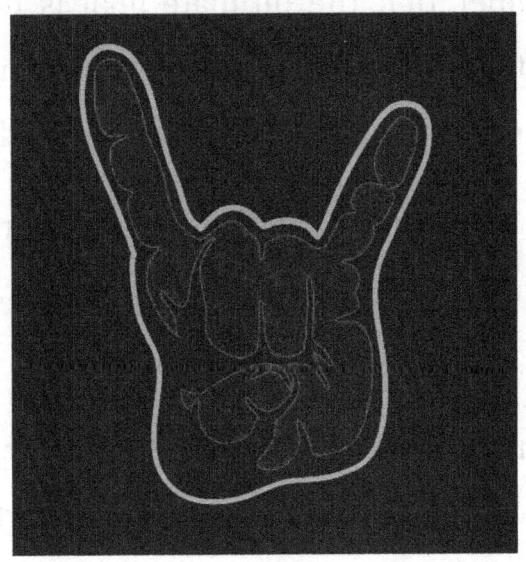

Recipes:

I come up with recipes that even a monkey could make. So I am sorry in advance for not having a lot of fluff and excitement that goes a long with any of my recipes (if you even can call them that). I am seriously just a simple man who likes my foods to be simple to prepare so that I can get on with my life and do the things that I love to do. Having said this, I still spend most of my time in the kitchen as it is, so I can only imagine how much time I would spend in the kitchen if I were to actually try and make elaborate fancy dishes that I really could not care any less about than I already do.

Here are a few smoothie recipes taken from some of my smoothie recipe books. Feel free to go and check them out if you are interested.

These are taken from **30 Delicious Blueberry Smoothies for Weight Loss & Body Detoxification** This book really did make the Amazon best sellers list for its category. And no, I am not just saying this like so many people do on Amazon. It really did.

Blueberry smoothie recipes

#1

2 cups of frozen organic blueberries.

1 large handful of baby spinach.

1 tablespoon of organic honey.

A teaspoon of cinnamon.

1 banana.

4 – 6 ounces of water.

Blend and enjoy!

This smoothie comes in at roughly around 357 calories, and has around 85 grams of carbs, 3 grams of protein, 1.5 grams of fat.

Blueberry smoothie recipe #2

1 cup of frozen organic blueberries.

1 large handful of baby spinach.

16 oz. of liquid egg whites.

A dash of 100% stevia.

Blend and enjoy!

This smoothie comes out to roughly around 288.5 calories, and has around 51 grams of protein, 20 grams of carbs, and a half a gram of fat.

Blueberry smoothie recipe #3

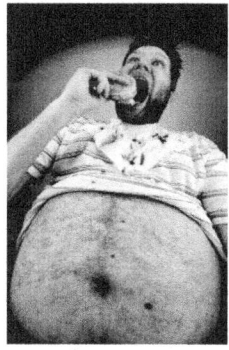

1 cup of frozen organic blueberries.

1 large handful of baby spinach.

16 oz. of liquid egg whites.

½ cup of frozen pineapple chunks.

A dash of 100% stevia.

Blend and enjoy!

This smoothie comes out to roughly around 328 calories, and has around 51 grams of protein, 30 grams of carbs, and a half a gram of fat.

Blueberry smoothie recipe #4

1 cup of frozen organic blueberries.

1 large handful of baby spinach.

½ cup of frozen mango chunks.

16 oz. of liquid egg whites.

A dash of 100% stevia.

Blend and enjoy!

This smoothie comes out to roughly around 338.5 calories, and has around 51 grams of protein, 32.5 grams of carbs, and a half a gram of fat.

Blueberry smoothie recipe #5:

1 cup of organic frozen blueberries.

1 large handful of baby spinach.

16 oz. of liquid egg whites.

1 banana.

A dash of 100% stevia.

Blend for a few seconds.

Add one tablespoon of natural peanut butter.

Blend and enjoy!

This smoothie comes out to roughly around 497 calories, and has around 56 grams of protein, 48 grams of carbs, 9 grams of fat.

Blueberry smoothie recipe #6

3 cups of organic frozen blueberries.

16 oz. of liquid egg whites.

1 banana.

Blend for a few seconds.

Add 1 tablespoon of natural peanut butter.

Blend and pour.

Then add a serving of coconut flakes on top.

Enjoy!

This smoothie comes out to roughly around 714 calories, and has around 57 grams of protein, 89 grams of carbs, 13 grams of fat.

These are taken from <u>Non Dairy Smoothie Recipes</u>.

Banana Mango

3 bananas.

1 cup of frozen mango chunks.

8 oz. of cranberry juice not from concentrate.

Some 100% stevia.

Possibly just a little bit of ice.

Blend and enjoy!

This smoothie comes out to roughly right around 489.5 calories, and has roughly around 116 grams of carbohydrates, 3 grams of protein, and 1.5 grams of fat.

Banana & Dates

3 bananas.

5 dates.

1 cup of frozen mango chunks.

6 – 8 oz. of water.

Possibly just a little ice.

Blend and enjoy!

This smoothie comes out to roughly right around 545.5 calories, and has got roughly around 130 carbohydrates, 3 grams of protein, and 1.5 grams of fat.

Banana Dates & Pineapple

3 bananas.

5 dates.

1 cup of frozen pineapple chunks.

6 – 8 oz. of water.

Possibly a little bit of ice.

Blend and enjoy!

This smoothie comes out to roughly right around 525.5 calories, and has around 125 grams of carbohydrates, 3 grams of protein, and 1.5 grams of fat.

Cranberry Hone

3 bananas.

5 dates.

1 tablespoon of organic honey.

8 oz. of cranberry juice not from concentrate.

A little 100% stevia.

Definitely some ice as to your liking.

Blend and enjoy!

This smoothie comes out to right around 589.5 calories, and has right around 141 grams of carbohydrates, 3 grams of protein, and 1.5 grams of fat.

Peanut Butter & Fruit

3 bananas.

5 dates.

1 tablespoon of organic honey.

1 tablespoon of natural peanut butter.

4 – 8 oz. of water.

A lot of ice.

Blend and enjoy!

This smoothie comes out to roughly right around 625.5 calories, and has roughly right around 128 grams of carbohydrates, 7 grams of protein, and 9.5 grams of fat.

Oat Smoothie

3 bananas.

5 dates.

½ cup of old fashioned oats.

4 – 8 oz. of water.

A lot of ice.

Blend and enjoy!

This smoothie comes out to right around 520.5 calories, and has got around 132 grams of carbs, 8 grams of protein, and 4.5 grams of fat.

Icey Dates

3 bananas.

10 dates.

4 – 8 oz. of water.

A lot of ice.

Blend and enjoy!

This smoothie comes out to right around 565.5 calories, and has roughly 135 grams of carbs, 3 grams of protein, and 1.5 grams of fat.

Banana Raisins

3 bananas.

½ cup of raisins.

4 – 8 oz. of water.

A lot of ice.

Blend and enjoy!

This smoothie comes out to roughly right around 565.5 calories, and has got roughly right around 133 grams of carbs, 5 grams of protein, and 1.5 grams of fat.

Cinnamon Raisin

3 bananas.

½ cup of raisins.

¼ cup of old fashioned oats.

A tablespoon of cinnamon.

4 – 8 oz. of water.

A lot of ice.

Blend and enjoy!

This smoothie comes out to roughly right around 640.5 calories, and has got roughly around 146.5 grams of carbs, 5.5 grams of protein, and 3 grams of fat.

Mango Heavy

3 bananas.

3 cups of frozen mango chunks.

A tablespoon of cinnamon.

8 oz. of water.

Blend and enjoy!

This smoothie comes out to right around 625.5 calories, and has got roughly around 150 grams of carbohydrates, 3 grams of protein, and 1.5 grams of fat.

Blueberry Cinnamon

2 cups of frozen mango chunks.

1 cup of frozen blueberries.

1 tablespoon of organic honey.

1 tablespoon of cinnamon.

4 – 8 oz. of water.

Blend and enjoy!

This smoothie comes out to roughly right around 368.5 calories, and has around 90 grams of carbs, 1 gram of protein, and a half a gram of fat.

Almond Milk Strawberry

2 cups of frozen mango chunks.

2 cups of frozen strawberries.

1 tablespoon of natural peanut butter.

6 oz. of almond milk.

Blend and enjoy!

This smoothie comes out to right around 500 calories, and has roughly 108 carbs, 4 grams of protein, and 8 grams of fat.

Mango Berry Cinnamon

2 cups of frozen mango chunks.

1 cup of frozen pineapple chunks.

1 cup of frozen blueberries.

1 banana.

1 tablespoon of cinnamon.

100% stevia.

4 – 8 oz. of water.

Blend and enjoy!

This smoothie comes out to right around 477 calories, and has roughly 115 grams of carbs, 2 grams of protein, and 1 gram of fat.

When it comes to cooking I like to take the easiest route possible. You would be amazed at what a 20$ rice cooker can do. When I cook my rice often I will throw in whatever vegetable that I feel like eating. Sometimes I feel like eating asparagus, so I will throw in asparagus with my rice and cook it. Sometimes I feel like having broccoli, so I will just dump in some broccoli with my rice and let it cook.

Quinoa cooks well in a rice maker also. Quinoa contains a complete source of protein that contains all of the essential amino acids that our bodies do not produce if this is of any interest to you.

I like quinoa sometimes. I have a hard time finding it at a reasonable price since it is right now one of the latest and greatest buzz word foods like coconut oil, kale, and a whole laundry list of others. But I will sometimes buy a pound or two and mix it with my rice.

I will just put a cup of dry rice in my rice maker with a cup of quinoa. Sometimes I will fill the top with veggies, and sometimes I wont. I just double the water as you would with rice and let the cooker do its job. And voila! In about a half an hour I have got a tasty dish that I can add whatever else I am eating with it and stuff my pie hole and fuel my body.

I love my rice cooker and cant believe that it took me till I was 36 years of age to finally buy one. I barely bought my first rice cooker last year. I used to make my rice on the stove the old fashioned way.

You can do so many things with a rice cooker like boil eggs, boil potatoes, cook oats, and even steam vegetables. I would definitely recommend putting a few bucks towards a rice cooker. Mine cost 20$ at Walmart on sale. I grabbed the last one that was in stock. I was actually just going there to purchase some socks and decided to take a stroll around the isles and see if I could find anything on clearance. I lucked out when I found the last rice cooker sitting all by itself on the bottom shelf. That was one of the best 20$ investments that I have ever made.

Here is a few pictures of basically what my meals look like. Very simple as I am just a simple minded individual.

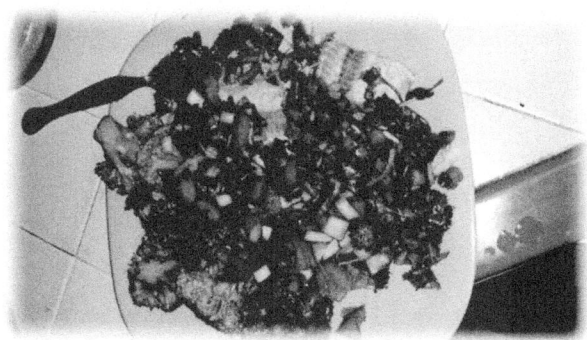

How to shop and eat right for under 50$ a week:

This is where I feel that I can best show people how to do this through a video. So what I am going to do is I am going to use the profits from this book here and save up to buy a cheap little video camera. If I don't make enough within a reasonable time I will just have to use my cell phone camera which kind of sucks but it will still do the job. I will make a YouTube video on this eventually and show exactly how I can eat for around 50$ a week. I eat big too. So someone who requires a smaller amount of calories than I do will be able to spend even less.

A family of 4 could eat healthy and keep the price down right around 100 - 120$ a week depending on how big the kids are and so forth. But it is not hard to do at all and the foods are going to be the healthiest foods that you can get in your stores.

I really don't understand how people don't just naturally lean towards this type of shopping since the staples that are the healthiest to eat are the cheapest. **Forget organic.** Organic foods are overpriced because they have become a marketing ploy. I used to be an organic freak, but lately I have done some of my own research on "organic" foods and I am not so much convinced anymore that they are worth the extra price tag that comes along with them.

Once I figure out exactly how I am going to be able to get past the embarrassment of walking around the store with a video camera looking like a self absorbed nit wit, I will make this video and probably put it up on YouTube and put a link in this book to the video.

If this is of any interest to you, then you will just have to check out my Authors page on Amazon as I will also put the link up somewhere in my bio or something like that. Check inside of the free preview of this book as well as I will put the link in the beginning of the book so that everyone who is just browsing can go click on the link and make fun of me on YouTube! I really don't feel like sticking my ugly mug in front of a camera but hey, if it helps out the cause and people can benefit from these videos then it is videos that I will try and do as well to go along with my books.

I bought all of this in that picture plus a little bag of frozen salmon fillets with the skins for 40$. The other 10$ I put into my carb staples which I buy in bulk. I buy 25 lbs. of rice at a time. I buy 10 even 20 lbs. of oats at a time. I actually ate this particular week for probably around 42$ considering that I buy my rice and oats in such big quantities, the price per serving comes out to just pennies. But I want to round up and leave a little wiggle room to play with.

I am a 200+ pound active guy who eats 3,000 calories a day minimum, so most people can even keep their weekly shopping bill down around or even below 40$ I guarantee it.

When I do these shopping videos I will do several of them and purchase different items each time to show just how easy it really is to eat for 50$ a week.

If I absolutely had to, I could cut out the egg whites and salmon which are my two most expensive items and go full blown vegan and still get in my 200+ grams of protein if I want to and maintain my 70/25/5 way of eating. I could even do a 60/25/15 pattern on a vegan diet if I wanted to.

If I went with a vegan diet I could eat 3,000+ calories and still keep the same macros all for under 40$ a week easy. I could probably go under 30$, but I will say 40$ just to be on the safe side. Maybe I will make videos on this as well.

I call myself a fishaterian. I mostly eat like a vegetarian but I like to throw fish into my diet from time to time. Mainly for the protein unless I am eating salmon which I like for the protein and also the good fats that are in salmon.

But I could go vegan if I had to no problem and do it right. Many people fail miserably trying to go vegan and even vegetarian because they have absolutely no clue what they are doing.

I am very much in tune with my body when it comes to diet. And the older that I get, the more my body leans towards a vegan eating style. A lot of these vegans are undernourished starving people who couldn't tell the hole in the ground from the hole in their own head when it comes to proper nutrition. These people are who give the vegan lifestyle a bad rap because everyone out in the real world looks at them as if they are grade A loony tunes (which most of them are). On the other end, vegetarianism and veganism have also been infiltrated by snake oil salesmen and savvy marketers who are using it only to pimp out worthless products and supplements to newbies. I would bet dollars to doughnuts that those people are eating doughnuts as they are counting all of their dollars they make off of naïve people who believe their hogwash.

Everything good in this world eventually gets ruined by marketers. These people are all over Amazon ruining this business that I am in right now as we speak. I am anti all of that.

When we are well fed and our bodies are running on a full tank of fuel our decision making when it comes to food choices becomes better. If we are super starving all the time we are going to pretty much eat anything that we can get our hands on. This is natures way of surviving.

You cant go wrong with any of the staples that I mentioned earlier even the canned foods. Make large amounts of staples like rice and beans and know what macros are inside of what you just made.

If you are trying to eat 150 grams of protein and 30 grams of fat a day then eat foods that allow you to be within those calorie ranges. If your body needs 150 grams of protein to run at its best, then there is no need for you to be eating 250 grams of protein. This is a huge waste of money as protein by itself is going to be the biggest expense when it comes to food.

The same thing goes with fat, if you can get all of your fat that you need a day from what is inside all of the carb sources that you eat a day, then there is absolutely no need to add extra fat into your foods.

Its all a balancing act that each person will have to figure out how to do on their own based on their bodies needs and also what they prefer to eat. Take 45$ only with you to the grocery store and try and pick out your proteins, fruits, and vegetables for the week. Leave out the carb staples. You can buy those in bulk separate from what you purchase with that 45$.

Now divvy it all up according to your bodies needs for each day during the week as best as you can. It may take several months to get it down to a science, but once you do it will become second nature to you.

You are going to the grocery store with a purpose. Your not just going in there willy nilly in order to browse the isles.

If you need 185 grams of protein a day, and you need to get 75 of those grams from protein only sources, and the rest are from what goes along with your carb staples, then you just figure 75 X 7 days in the week which comes out to 525 grams of protein that you need to come from protein sources only for the entire week.

Now only you can decide where it is that you are going to get not only the best bang for your buck, but also the best sources of that protein from.

You are only going to find that ratio of protein to fat to carbs in an animal product. Now you are going to have to read labels and find out which animal products are that lean. I already told you the absolute two leanest which are liquid egg whites, and canned tuna in water. You will not find any other protein sources that come with any less fat and carbs than these two sources come with.

I cant make your decision for you, but lets say that you decided to go with canned tuna in water as your protein for the week. Well you need to get 525 total grams of protein coming from the tuna. There is roughly about 20 grams of protein in a small can of tuna depending on the brand. So 525 divided by 20 comes out to around 26 cans of tuna for the week roughly. So basically you are going to be eating 3.5 cans of tuna a day roughly. I am just rounding this stuff off here so please all you math wizards out there don't ream me out for not being so technical.

When you shop for tuna always look at the price per ounce rather than the total price of the container that it comes in. It is not always cheaper to buy the bigger tin cans of tuna rather than the smaller ones per ounce for some reason. I have noticed this a lot with tuna. Usually with most everything else the bigger quantity that you buy at once the cheaper it is per serving. But for some reason this is not always the case with tuna, so always compare tuna by the price per ounce. Tuna is always on sale and sometimes you can find 4 ounce cans of tuna for as low as 50 cents. But for the most part a 4 ounce can of tuna will usually cost right around 1$ each. So your protein for the week is going to cost you around 26$. Not too bad huh?

Now that 19$ that is remaining is going to be going towards your fruits and vegetables for the week.

Now like I said, I never count my vegetable calories and I eat however many I feel like when I feel like eating them, which is a lot of vegetables that I consume a day.

But I do count my fruits as macros. When it comes down to your fruits and veggies for the week try and stretch out that remaining 19$ as far as you possibly can stretch it.

If you have a little extra left and the prices are right in your area throw in some sweet potatoes or yams and use them as a staple carb just to break up the monotony of whatever it is that your main carb staple is.

Just keep practicing every week and try and become more efficient with your grocery shopping. Like I said after a while it really does become second nature. If there were no one in the store at all I could go in and get all of my food that I need for the week in the basket in less than 2 minutes easy. I am also like a magician with the hand baskets as well. I can fit 20 lbs. of potatoes into a 10 lb. hand basket and still have room to pull a rabbit out of the bottom of it.

The girls at the cash register are always amazed at how much food I can fit into one of those little hand baskets. One day I am going to put a little toy rabbit in the bottom and have them pull it out at the register. But I bet they wouldn't get the joke and look at me as if I were just another weirdo (which I sort of am) they have to pretend to be nice to in the store.

Prepare your food ahead of time:

I am telling you that life is so much easier when you get into a habit of preparing your food way ahead of time. Especially your breakfast. At least this is the case for me. I am almost obsessed with making sure that I have my food prepared way ahead of time. It has been years since I have had to wake up and prepare my breakfast. I am in the habit of getting my breakfast ready the night before and I would feel weird now if I didn't do it.

I am one of those anti microwave weirdos, but don't worry I wont judge you if you use one. But my friendly advice would be to take your microwave to the landfill. Or better yet, take it and donate it to a homeless shelter where they can make some good use out of it.

I definitely recommend at least preparing your breakfast the night before if not all of your meals for the next day the night before. This keeps you feeding and fueling your body with no interruptions or distractions. I know how people are. All that it takes is one little monkey wrench to be thrown into their lives and they are back at the fast food joint getting the 99 cent wonder meat taco, or the 2 for 1 cheese burger deal.

Keep all of your meals with you at all times for the day. Carry around a good insulated lunch box. Don't ever paper bag it. Buy a really good **BIG** insulted lunch box. Keep your meals in Tupperware containers and keep your food cold with ice packs if you have to. What is wrong with eating your food cold? If you don't have the luxury of being near a refrigerator and a stove all day long (and this is most people with jobs) then this is what you are going to have to do. Just suck it up and convince yourself to enjoy it. It is all fuel that your body needs, so think of it as that. And give it the best fuel possible so that you can perform at your best on all cylinders.

Conclusion:

Hang out with me on Instagram @dextersworld

Well I tried my best here to combine a healthy way of eating all while living on a small budget. I hope that I could help out even if it was just a little bit. I am always going to base all of my books on real world nutrition no matter what. These are my beliefs and I all I can really do, is show you how I do things. I cant make anyone do anything that they do not want to do. If you enjoyed the read and felt as if you got some benefit from it, then think that you could possibly go back on Amazon and review it for me? Reviews are so hard to come by and I would appreciate it greatly.

Carpe Diem

Dexter

Hold on! I have some more recipes for you, just because you're an awesome person.

These are from one of my latest recipe books in July of 2017. I hope that you can implement some of these into your personal eating style. Enjoy!

Rice Cooker VEGAN Recipes

50 Vegan Recipes Total
20 Quinoa Recipes

Easy Meal Prep - Plant Based Cooking

Dexter Poin

Fruit and Bean Quinoa Salad

Serves: 8

Time: 35 minutes

Ingredients:
- 1 cup quinoa
- 2 cups water
- 1 orange juice
- 1 lime juice
- 12 jalapeno pepper, minced
- 1/4 cup fresh mint, minced
- 1/4 cup fresh cilantro, minced
- 1 red bell pepper, diced
- 1 1/2 cups black beans, cooked and drained
- 1 1/2 cups avocado, peel and diced

- 2 cups mango, diced
- 2 tbsp balsamic vinegar
- 2 tbsp olive oil
- 1/2 tsp salt
- Pepper

Directions:

1. Add quinoa, water, and salt in a rice cooker. Stir well and cook for 15 minutes.
2. After 15 minutes fluff the quinoa using fork and transfer in large mixing bowl.
3. Combine together vinegar and olive oil.
4. Add vinegar and olive oil mixture to the quinoa and mix well and set aside to cool.
5. Once quinoa is cool then add orange juice, lime juice, jalapeno pepper, mint, cilantro, red bell pepper, black beans, avocado, and mangoes. Toss well.
6. Season salad with pepper and salt.
7. Serve and enjoy.

Nutritional Value (Amount per Serving):

- Calories 357

- Fat 11 g
- Carbohydrates 55 g
- Sugar 14 g
- Protein 12 g
- Cholesterol 0 mg

Cranberry Kale Quinoa

Serves: 1

Time: 25 minutes

Ingredients:

- 1/3 cup quinoa, rinsed and drained
- 2 tbsp orange juice
- 1 tbsp olive oil
- 1/3 cup cranberries, dried
- 1/2 cup kale, chopped
- 2/3 cup water
- 1/4 tsp cinnamon
- Pepper
- Salt

Directions:

1. Add quinoa, orange juice, olive oil, cranberries, kale, and water in rice cooker. Stir well.
2. Turn on rice cooker and cook quinoa for 20 minutes. Stir 2 to 3 times.
3. Once it cooks then add cinnamon, pepper, and salt. Stir well.
4. Serve and enjoy.

Nutritional Value (Amount per Serving):
- Calories 381
- Fat 17 g
- Carbohydrates 47 g
- Sugar 4 g
- Protein 9 g
- Cholesterol 0 mg

Easy Quinoa Porridge

Serves: 2

Time: 20 minutes

Ingredients:

- 1/2 cup quinoa, rinsed and drained
- 1 cup water
- 1/4 cup almonds, chopped
- 1 medium apple, diced
- 1 cup almond milk
- 1/2 cup rolled oats
- 1 tbsp maple syrup

Directions:

1. Add quinoa, oats, almond milk, and water in rice cooker and stir well.

2. Seal rice cooker with lid and cook for 15 minutes.
3. Once it cooked then open lid and stirs quinoa mixture well.
4. Add quinoa in two bowls and top with chopped almonds, apple, and maple syrup.
5. Serve warm and enjoy.

Nutritional Value (Amount per Serving):
- Calories 663
- Fat 38 g
- Carbohydrates 72 g
- Sugar 22 g
- Protein 14 g
- Cholesterol 0 mg

Simple Garlic Quinoa

Serves: 4

Time: 35 minutes

Ingredients:

- 2 cups quinoa, rinsed and drained
- 1/2 cup onion, chopped
- 1/2 tsp garlic, minced
- 1 tbsp olive oil
- 2 1/2 cups vegetable broth

Directions:

1. Add olive in the rice cooker and select sauté.
2. Add onion and garlic and sauté for 3 minutes.
3. Add quinoa and stir for 1 minute.
4. Pour vegetable broth in the rice cooker and stir well.

5. Cook quinoa in the rice cooker for 25 minutes.
6. Using fork fluff the quinoa and serve.

Nutritional Value (Amount per Serving):

- Calories 373
- Fat 9 g
- Carbohydrates 56 g
- Sugar 1 g
- Protein 15 g
- Cholesterol 0 mg

Quinoa Broccoli Casserole

Serves: 4

Time: 30 minutes

Ingredients:

- 1 1/2 cups quinoa, rinsed and drained
- 1 lemon juice
- 1 tbsp vegan butter
- 4 garlic cloves, minced
- 1 small head broccoli, chopped
- 1/4 cup vegan cheese
- 3 cups water
- Pepper

- Salt

Directions:
1. Add butter in the rice cooker and select sauté.
2. Once butter is melted then add garlic and stir for 30 seconds.
3. Add quinoa in the rice cooker and stir well.
4. Now water and lemon juice and seal cooker with lid.
5. Once the half liquid is absorbed then open the lid and stir quinoa well.
6. Add chopped broccoli on top of quinoa and cover rice cooker with lid again.
7. Once the broccoli is cooked then open the lid. Add cheese and stir well until cheese is melted.
8. Serve and enjoy.

Nutritional Value (Amount per Serving):
- Calories 290
- Fat 8 g
- Carbohydrates 44 g
- Sugar 0.4 g
- Protein 10 g
- Cholesterol 8 mg

Healthy Quinoa Salad

Serves: 6

Time: 40 minutes

Ingredients:

- For salad:
- 1/2 cup quinoa, rinsed and drained
- 2/3 cup water
- 1/4 cup vegan cheese, crumbled
- 1/2 cup cherry tomatoes, sliced
- 1/2 cup cranberries, dried
- 1/2 cup cucumbers, sliced
- 1/2 cup peas
- For dressing:
- 1 tbsp shallot, chopped
- 1 tbsp lemon juice
- 1 tsp lemon zest

- 1 tbsp vinegar
- 2 tbsp olive oil
- 1/4 tsp pepper

Directions:

1. Add water and quinoa in the rice cooker and cook on the quick cook.
2. Meanwhile, in a small bowl combine together all dressing ingredients.
3. Once quinoa is cooked then fluff with a fork and add in large mixing bowl. Set aside quinoa for 5 minutes to cool.
4. Now add tomatoes, cranberries, cucumbers, peas and cheese.
5. Pour dressing over salad and toss well.
6. Serve immediately and enjoy.

Nutritional Value (Amount per Serving):

- Calories 125
- Fat 6 g
- Carbohydrates 13 g
- Sugar 1 g
- Protein 3 g
- Cholesterol 0 mg

Blueberry Breakfast Quinoa

Serves: 4

Time: 30 minutes

Ingredients:

- 1 cup quinoa, rinsed and drained
- 1 cup blueberries
- 1 tsp cinnamon
- 1/2 tsp cloves
- 1 tsp nutmeg
- 2 tbsp sugar
- 1 tsp vanilla extract
- 2 cup almond milk, unsweetened

Directions:

1. Using fork mash blueberries.

2. Add all ingredients into the rice cooker and stir well.
3. Cook quinoa mixture on white rice setting.
4. Stir well and serve.

Nutritional Value (Amount per Serving):

- Calories 484
- Fat 31 g
- Carbohydrates 46 g
- Sugar 13 g
- Protein 9 g
- Cholesterol 0 mg

Green Beans Quinoa

Serves: 4

Time: 30 minutes

Ingredients:

- 1 cup quinoa, rinsed and drained
- 1 1/3 cup water
- 1/2 cup cashews, roasted
- 3 tbsp vinaigrette
- 1 medium tomato, cored and chopped
- 12 oz green beans, remove stems and chopped
- 1 tsp salt

Directions:

1. Add quinoa, salt, and water in rice cooker. Stir well and start rice cooker on white rice setting.

2. Once quinoa starts boiling then add green beans on steamer rack and place steamer over quinoa.
3. Cover and cook green beans for 5 minutes.
4. After 5 minutes remove steamer and cook quinoa continue for total 15 minutes.
5. Using fork fluff the quinoa and place in large mixing bowl.
6. Add chopped tomatoes, steamed green beans, and vinaigrette in quinoa and toss well.
7. Top quinoa with cashews and serve.

Nutritional Value (Amount per Serving):
- Calories 341
- Fat 16 g
- Carbohydrates 40 g
- Sugar 3 g
- Protein 10 g
- Cholesterol 0 mg

Tasty Red Quinoa with Rice

Serves: 4

Time: 30 minutes

Ingredients:

- 1/2 cup red quinoa, rinsed and drained
- 3 cups water
- 1 cup rice, rinsed and drained
- 1 tbsp olive oil
- 1/4 tsp salt

Directions:

1. Add all ingredients into the rice cooker and stir well.
2. Start rice cooker.
3. Once rice cooker rice setting changes to warm then open the lid.

4. Stir well and serve.

Nutritional Value (Amount per Serving):

- Calories 284
- Fat 4 g
- Carbohydrates 54 g
- Sugar 0.6 g
- Protein 5 g
- Cholesterol 0 mg

Kale Raisin Quinoa

Serves: 1

Time: 30 minutes

Ingredients:

- 1/3 cup quinoa, rinsed and drained
- 1 cup kale, chopped
- 1/4 cup almond milk
- 1/2 tsp cinnamon
- 3 tbsp raisins
- 2/3 cup water
- 1/4 tsp salt

Directions:

1. Add quinoa, water, salt, cinnamon, and raisins in the rice cooker and stir well.
2. Start rice cooker. When rice cooker goes on warm mode then open the lid and stir well.

3. Add kale and almond milk and stir well and set it in warm mode for 5 minutes.
4. Serve and enjoy.

Nutritional Value (Amount per Serving):
- Calories 464
- Fat 17 g
- Carbohydrates 69 g
- Sugar 18 g
- Protein 12 g
- Cholesterol 0 mg

Mixed Vegetable Quinoa

Serves: 4

Time: 30 minutes

Ingredients:

- 1 cup quinoa, rinsed and drained
- 2 tbsp liquid amino
- 1 tbsp sesame oil
- 2 cup mixed vegetables
- 3 cups vegetable broth

Directions:

1. Add vegetable broth and quinoa in the rice cooker and stir well.
2. Add vegetables to steamer basket and place over quinoa.
3. Cook quinoa on white rice setting. It takes 20 minutes to cook.

4. Once cooking finish then adds quinoa and vegetable in large mixing bowl.
5. Add liquid amino and sesame oil in quinoa and vegetable mixture and stir well.
6. Serve warm and enjoy.

Nutritional Value (Amount per Serving):
- Calories 259
- Fat 7 g
- Carbohydrates 37 g
- Sugar 0.5 g
- Protein 12 g
- Cholesterol 0 mg

Delicious Lentil Quinoa

Serves: 4

Time: 30 minutes

Ingredients:

- 1 1/2 cups quinoa, rinsed and drained
- 5 cups water
- 1/2 cup green lentils
- 1/4 tsp basil
- 1/4 tsp chili powder
- 1 tsp paprika

Directions:

1. Add all ingredients into the rice cooker and stir well.
2. Cook lentil quinoa mixture on white rice setting. About 20 minutes.
3. Stir well and serve.

Nutritional Value (Amount per Serving):

- Calories 322
- Fat 4 g
- Carbohydrates 55 g
- Sugar 0.6 g
- Protein 15 g
- Cholesterol 0 mg

Yummy Fruit and Quinoa Salad

Serves: 10

Time: 30 minutes

Ingredients:

- 2 cups quinoa
- 1 1/2 tbsp fresh mint, chopped
- 3/4 cups pecans, toasted and chopped
- 1 medium orange, peeled and sliced
- 1 apple, cored, peel and diced
- 1 mango, peel, pitted and chopped
- 2 1/4 cups water
- 2 tsp cinnamon
- 1 tbsp maple syrup

Directions:

1. Add water and quinoa in a rice cooker.

2. Start rice cooker and select brown rice setting.
3. Once quinoa is cooked then transfer quinoa in mixing bowl.
4. Now add all remaining ingredients into the quinoa bowl and toss well.
5. Serve and enjoy.

Nutritional Value (Amount per Serving):
- Calories 221
- Fat 7 g
- Carbohydrates 34 g
- Sugar 10 g
- Protein 6 g
- Cholesterol 0 mg

Spinach kale Chickpeas Quinoa

Serves: 5

Time: 1 hour 10 minutes

Ingredients:

- 1 cup quinoa, rinsed and drained
- 2 cups water
- 6 tbsp fresh lemon juice
- 3 tbsp olive oil
- 1 cup cranberries, dried
- 1 cup chickpeas, soaked overnight and drained
- 1 1/2 cups spinach, chopped
- 1 1/2 cups kale, chopped

Directions:

1. Add all ingredients into the rice cooker and stir well.
2. Start rice cooker and cook quinoa mixture.

3. Stir quinoa mixture two times while cooking.
4. Stir well and serve.

Nutritional Value (Amount per Serving):
- Calories 371
- Fat 13 g
- Carbohydrates 50 g
- Sugar 5 g
- Protein 13 g
- Cholesterol 0 mg

Pomegranate Mint Quinoa Salad

Serves: 8

Time: 30 minutes

Ingredients:

- 2 cups quinoa, rinsed and drained
- 1/2 cup fresh mint, chopped
- 1/2 tsp all spice powder
- 1 cup pomegranate seeds
- 4 cups water
- 1 tbsp olive oil
- 2 tbsp fresh lemon juice
- 1/4 cup pine nuts, toasted
- 1/4 tsp salt

Directions:

1. Add quinoa, salt, and water in rice cooker and stir well.
2. Turn on rice cooker and cook quinoa on white rice setting.
3. Once quinoa is cooked then using fork fluff the quinoa and place in large mixing bowl.
4. Add lemon juice and all spice powder in quinoa and stir well.
5. Now add all remaining ingredients into the quinoa bowl and toss well.
6. Serve and enjoy.

Nutritional Value (Amount per Serving):

- Calories 216
- Fat 7 g
- Carbohydrates 28 g
- Sugar 0.2 g
- Protein 7 g
- Cholesterol 0 mg

Turmeric Curry Quinoa

Serves: 4

Time: 30 minutes

Ingredients:

- 1 cup quinoa, rinsed and drained
- 3/4 cup water
- 1/2 tsp paprika
- 1 tsp garlic pepper
- 1 tsp ground turmeric
- 1 tsp curry powder
- 2 tbsp garlic powder
- 2 tbsp parsley, dried
- 2 tbsp onion flakes, dried
- 1 1/2 cups tomatoes, chopped

Directions:

1. Add all ingredients into the rice cooker and cook until all liquid is absorbed.

2. Stir well and serve.

Nutritional Value (Amount per Serving):

- Calories 196
- Fat 3 g
- Carbohydrates 36 g
- Sugar 3 g
- Protein 7 g
- Cholesterol 0 mg

Easy Steel Cut Oats

Serves: 6

Time: 30 minutes

Ingredients:

- 1 cup steel cut oats
- 1/2 cup almond milk
- 1/2 tsp cinnamon
- 3 1/2 cups water
- 1/2 cup bulgur, rinsed and drained
- 1 cup rolled oats

Directions:

1. Add oats, bulgur, salt and water in rice cooker and stir well.
2. Turn on rice cooker and cook oats mixture until all liquid absorbed.
3. Once it cooked then stir in almond milk and cinnamon.

4. Top oats with your choice topping and serve.

Nutritional Value (Amount per Serving):
- Calories 131
- Fat 2 g
- Carbohydrates 24 g
- Sugar 2 g
- Protein 5 g
- Cholesterol 0 mg

Simple Plain Quinoa

Serves: 4

Time: 40 minutes

Ingredients:

- 1 cup quinoa, rinsed and drained
- 14 oz vegetable broth
- Olive oil
- Salt

Directions:

1. Add all ingredients into the rice cooker and stir well.
2. Start rice cooker and cook quinoa until all liquid absorbed.
3. Using fork fluff the quinoa and serve.

Nutritional Value (Amount per Serving):

- Calories 172
- Fat 3 g
- Carbohydrates 27 g
- Sugar 0.3 g
- Protein 8 g
- Cholesterol 0 mg

Yummy Apple Quinoa

Serves: 1

Time: 25 minutes

Ingredients:

- 1/4 cup quinoa, rinsed and drained
- 1/4 cup water
- 1 tsp cinnamon
- 1/2 tbsp lemon juice
- 1 small apple, cored and chopped

Directions:

1. Add apple, cinnamon, water and lemon juice in a blender and blend until smooth.
2. Add apple mixture and quinoa in the rice cooker and stir well.
3. Start rice cooker and cook quinoa until liquid absorbed.

4. Stir well and serve.

Nutritional Value (Amount per Serving):

- Calories 280
- Fat 3 g
- Carbohydrates 60 g
- Sugar 23 g
- Protein 6 g
- Cholesterol 0 mg

Have you ever read any of my Rice Rice Baby books?
How about my fiction, and poetry writings?
No?
Well, if your interested in the fiction shtuff of mine, just message me, and ill lead you to where they can be found.

But, heres some more recipes for you, from some of my Rice Rice Baby series.

Check them out on Amazon. Rice Rice Baby #1 has sold tens of thousands of copies, all across this beautiful globe. And still selling to this very day! I hope you enjoy some of these recipes.

Rice Cooker Sushi

Ingredients

- 1 cup sticky rice
- 2 cups water
- 3 oz rice wine vinegar
- ½ teaspoon salt

Preparation

1. Cook the rice with water and salt. Let it sit for another 15minutes before opening the lid.

2. Now lay the rice in a dish and pour the vinegar on top of it. Use this rice mixture to roll up a sushi.

Serving

When you fill this mixture in a sushi sheet, drizzle some lemon juice on it.

Variation

You can use normal rice instead of sticky rice.

Rose Flavored Rice Pudding

Ingredients

- 1 cup rice (soaked)
- 1 cup almond milk
- ¼ teaspoon cardamom powder
- ½ teaspoon rose essence
- 1 teaspoon olive oil

Preparation

1. In a rice cooker, sauté the rice in oil for 6 minutes.

2. Add all the ingredients except rose essence and cook for one cycle for 20 minutes.

Serving

Serve this pudding slightly chilled and garnish with cashews and rose petals.

Variation

Rose essence can be replaced by vanilla essence.

Veggie Rice

Ingredients

- 1 cup rice (soaked)
- ¼ cup diced carrots
- ¼ cup finely chopped French beans
- ½ cup green peas (frozen)
- ¼ cup diced potatoes
- 1 tablespoon ginger garlic paste
- 1 bay leaf
- 2 cloves
- 2 cardamoms

- 1 tablespoon salt
- 1 teaspoon olive oil
- 2.5 cups water

Preparation

1. In a rice cooker, take some oil, add ginger garlic paste, onions and all the vegetables. Saute them for 7 minutes.

2. Add the rest of the ingredients and cook.

Serving

Serve in a large dish with coriander leaves or mint sprigs on top.

Variation

You can replace or add some more vegetables.

Black Bean Soup

Ingredients

- 1 cup black beans (cooked)
- ¼ cup carrots
- 2 finely chopped tomatoes
- 1 teaspoon lemon juice
- 3 minced garlic cloves
- 1 onion finely chopped
- 2 tablespoons red wine vinegar
- 1 teaspoon black pepper
- ¾ tablespoon salt

- ½ cup soaked rice
- 1.5 cups water

Preparation

1. In a rice cooker, sauté the garlic, onions, tomatoes and carrots for a while.
2. Add the rest of the ingredients and cook.

Serving

Serve in a shallow dish and garnish with mint sprigs.

Variation

You can also make a chick pea soup using the same remaining ingredients.

Yellow Dal

Ingredients

1. 1 cup chick pea dal
2. 1 onion finely chopped+1 onion thinly sliced.
3. 1 teaspoon ginger (shredded)
4. 4 minced garlic cloves
5. 1 teaspoon cumin powder and whole cumin
6. 2 mild green chilies
7. 1 teaspoon tamarind paste
8. 1 teaspoon olive oil

9. 2 cups water

Preparation

1. In a rice cooker, sauté chilies, ginger, garlic and onion for about 7 minutes.

2. Now add the rest of the ingredients and cook.

Serving

It is best served hot and with coriander leaves on top.

Variation

Instead of chick pea dal, you can use any other dal.

Couscous With Kale and Potatoes

Ingredients

- 1 cup couscous
- 2 diced potatoes
- 9-10 leaves of kale (chopped)
- 1 cup vegetable stock
- 1 teaspoon cumin
- 1 ½ tablespoon lemon juice
- ½ teaspoon lemon zest
- 1 teaspoon parsley
- ¾ tablespoon salt

- ½ teaspoon oil

Preparation

1. Sauté the potatoes, couscous, cumin and kale leaves for a 4-5 minutes.

2. Add remaining ingredients and cook for 30-35 minutes.

Serving

Serve it in a glass ware

Variation

Brown rice can be used instead of couscous.

Quinoa With Almonds and Corn

Ingredients

- 1 cup quinoa
- 1 diced carrot
- ½ cup sweet corn
- 8-9 almonds
- 7-8 finely chopped kale leaves
- 1 teaspoon salt
- 2 cups water
- 1 teaspoon paprika powder

Preparation

1. Wash and drain the water from quinoa.//
2. In a rice cooker, combine all the ingredients, cover the lid and cook for 45 minutes.

Serving

Serve this dish with sliced avocadoes and tempeh sticks.

Variation

You can also add chopped pineapple to get that tangy and sweet taste.

Mushroom and Black Bean Rice

Ingredients

- 1 cup shitake and button mushrooms (diced)
- 1 cup long grain rice
- ½ cup cooked black beans
- 1 finely chopped onion
- 3 minced garlic cloves
- 1 1/2 teaspoon oil (olive or coconut)
- 2 tablespoons onion powder
- 2 cups water
- ¾ tablespoon salt

Preparation

1. Sauté the garlic and onions in the rice cooker with some oil.

2. Add the remaining ingredients and cook for up to 25 minutes.

Serving

Serve with some coriander leaves.

Variation

Brown rice can be used instead of white rice.

Coconut Scented Rice With Roasted Almonds

Ingredients

- 1 cup white rice
- 2 cups coconut milk
- ¼ cup shaved coconut (fresh)
- 8-9 almonds
- ½ teaspoon cardamom powder
- ½ tablespoon salt

Preparation

1. Combine all the ingredients except almonds and cover with a lid.

2. Let the rice cook until about 25 minutes. Now roast the almonds on a pan until crisp and drizzle them over the rice.

Serving

Serve this yummy dish with some fresh cherries on top.

Variation

You can use sugar, stevia, or honey, if you you want a sweet rice.

Peanut Rice With Bell Peppers

Ingredients

- 3 finely chopped bell peppers (red, yellow and green)
- 1 cup soaked white rice
- 1 finely chopped onion
- ¼ cup peanut butter
- ¼ cup tomato puree
- 1 teaspoon paprika powder
- 1 teaspoon salt
- 2 cups water

1. Mix the peanut butter in some water and set aside. Now combine all the ingredients in a rice cooker and pour the peanut butter mixture over it.

2. Cook this rice for 30 minutes on medium heat.

Serving

Serve this rice a large white plate and garnish with mint sprigs

Lentils Kale and Miso Soup

Ingredients

- ½ cup lentils
- 7-8 finely chopped kale leaves
- ¼ cup sweet corn
- 1 tablespoon of Miso paste
- 1 teaspoon salt
- 1 minced garlic clove
- ½ teaspoon pepper powder
- 1 cup water

Preparation

1. Combine all the ingredients and cover with a lid.

2. Cook the soup for 20 minutes on medium heat.

Serving

Serve the soup with some fried noodles on top.

Variation

You can skip the sweet corn if you do not like them.

Apple and Raisin Porridge Rice

<u>Ingredients</u>

- 1 cup rice
- 1 finely chopped apple
- 1 cup apple juice
- ½ teaspoon cardamom
- 7-8 raisins
- 7-8 chopped cashews
- 5 tablespoons brown sugar
- 1 cup water

Preparation

1. Mix all the ingredients together along with the apple juice and cover the lid

2. Cook on medium flame for about 30-35 minutes.

Serving

Serve the porridge with roasted almonds on top.

Variation

You can cook the porridge using coconut milk instead of apple juice.

Creamy Mushroom Soup

Ingredients

- 1 cup diced button mushrooms
- 1 sliced onion
- 2 minced garlic cloves
- ¼ cup coconut milk
- ½ cup water
- 1 teaspoon salt
- ½ teaspoon pepper
- 1 teaspoon oil

Preparation:

1. In a slow cooker, sauté the garlic, onion, mushrooms and add the rest of the ingredients to it except coconut milk.

2. Cook this soup for 20 minutes in the rice cooker. Once cooled down, blend the mixture using a hand blender.

3. Add coconut milk to it and let it boil for 9-10 minutes.

Serving

Serve this soup in a big soup bowl with some chopped lemon grass on top.

Variation

If you do not wish to use coconut milk, you can simple use water.

Spicy Brown Rice Wraps

Ingredients

- 1 cup brown rice (half cooked)
- ¼ cup black beans (cooked)
- ¼ cup corn kernels
- 2 finely chopped tomatoes
- 1 finely chopped onion
- 2 green chilies (finely chopped)
- ¾ tablespoon salt
- 1 chopped avocado
- ½ teaspoon lemon juice

- 2 cups water
- 1 teaspoon oil (coconut oil)
- 4 or 5 tortillas

Preparation

1. Sauté the onions, tomato and green chilies with some oil in a rice cooker.
2. Add remaining ingredients and cook the rice for about 35 minutes.

Serving

Fill this mixture into tortillas one by one and secure them using toothpick.

Variation

You can fill this mixture inside hot dog buns and serve.

Spicy and Sour Sweet Potatoes

Ingredients

- 1.5 cups peeled and diced sweet potatoes
- 2 green chilies
- 1 tablespoon tamarind paste
- 1 teaspoon cumin
- 1 ½ teaspoon salt
- 1 bay leaf
- 1 teaspoon sesame seeds
- 1 cup water

- 1 teaspoon oil (olive or coconut)

Preparation

1. Take some oil in the rice cooker and sauté the cumin, green chilies and sweet potatoes in it for 6 minutes.

2. Add the remaining ingredients and cook for 20 minutes.

Serving

Serve it hot.

Variation

You can replace the sweet potatoes with regular potatoes.

Disclaimer:

The information in this book is to be read for entertainment purposes only. The information provided by the Author is not intended to be treatment or used as treatment for any type of illnesses. The Author and Publisher are not responsible for any person's safety and misjudgment of treatments. Always seek and consult with a trained and licensed healthcare provider. This is not to be viewed as a substitute for medical advice. No part of this book is to be removed and used as ones own without the written permission of the Author. Doing so would be considered an illegal act, and legal action will be taken accordingly.

Made in the USA
Monee, IL
03 May 2026

49437797R00148